MARTIN YAN QUICK & EASY

MARTIN YAN
QUICK & EASY

Photographs by Sheri Giblin and Stephanie Liu Jan

CHRONICLE BOOKS
SAN FRANCISCO

Library of Congress Cataloging-in-Publication Data:

Yan, Martin, 1948–
    Martin Yan quick & easy / Martin Yan; photographs by Sheri Giblin and Stephanie Liu Jan.
        p. cm.
    Includes index.
    ISBN 0-8118-4447-1 (pbk.)
1. Cookery, Asian. 2. Quick and easy cookery. I. Title: Quick and easy. II. Jan, Stephanie Liu. III. Title.
    TX724.5.A1Y3597 2004
    641.5′55′095—dc22
            2004005719

Manufactured in China.

Designed by Ph.D
Typesetting by Ph.D
Prop styling by Leigh Noe
Food styling by Dan Becker
Photographer's Assistant: Selena Aument

Distributed in Canada by Raincoast Books
9050 Shaughnessy Street
Vancouver, British Columbia V6P 6E5

10 9 8 7 6 5 4 3 2 1

Chronicle Books LLC
85 Second Street
San Francisco, California 94105

www.chroniclebooks.com

Yan Can Cook™ and the Yan Can Cook logos are trademarks of Yan Can Cook, Inc.

A La Carte Communications® is a registered trademark of Reunion Communications Corporation. All Rights Reserved.
http://www.alacartetv.com

ACKNOWLEDGMENTS

Once you know how, cooking Asian food can be quick and easy. Writing a book and making a TV series about the ease of Asian cooking is, however, a bit more complicated. But just like mastering Asian cooking, success comes from good planning and assembling all the right ingredients. For this project, I am blessed to have the dedication of my Yan Can Cook team, and the production talents of A La Carte Communications. Their creative energy and endless hours of hard work make this "Quick & Easy" vision a reality.

As always, the support of our wonderful and generous sponsors was crucial. Alan Chang and Batty Tsang at Lee Kum Kee (USA) have been with us through the years; and it's hard to think of quick and easy Asian cooking without thinking of Lee Kum Kee sauces. Sunkist Growers joined us for this project; and, of course, their citrus products are a critical component in my cooking. I especially want to thank Kellie DuBois at Sunkist for her enthusiastic support. GE Monogram — represented by Paul Klein, Nolan Pike, Randall Fong, and Marty Troian — returned to support the show and provided their brilliantly designed kitchen appliances as well as an appreciation of our cooking. Florence Sheffer and Suzanne Howard of Meyer Corporation joined us again with their Circulon cookware line, which has always been an invaluable part of our kitchen. Howard Ong brought back Aroma Housewares, makers of fabulous rice cookers, as a repeat sponsor. Jim Bellrose and Lanny Chase, of Dexter-Russell Cutlery, joined us this season; and I was privileged to be able to use their fine knives. Joe Hernandez and Nancy Eisman brought back sponsorship from Melissa's World, a produce line that is indispensable for Asian cooking. Michael Mendez and Tim Cannon from Diamond of California have been enthusiastic supporters for several years; their nuts are so important to Asian recipes. Tai Foong seafood and Asian gourmet products, represented by Gary Merritt and my friend Davy Lam, joined us for this season. And Cindy Turk at Maple Leaf Farms has been as enthusiastic about the series as I am about their duck products.

We covered many miles for this series. From Taiwan to my home province of Guangzhau (formerly Canton) in mainland China, and to many scenic spots along the majestic Yangtze River. It was a journey filled with eye-opening and mouth-watering adventures. Our success would not have been possible without the outstanding on-site support from Taiwan Tourism, ably represented by Ms. Jane Huang and Ms. Emily Yi-Ping Huang, who provided critical access to places throughout that beautiful island. In China, Mr. Shao Guang He, Mr. Simon Ho, and Ms. Nina Li are successful Guangzhou broadcasters and entrepreneurs, who were superb hosts. Along the Yangtze we had the joy of traveling with Viking River Cruises, who treated us like royalty and made all of their considerable resources available to us.

As we traveled, we had the support of first-rate crews everywhere we went. Dan Dominy was especially important in capturing what we saw; and he was ably assisted by Ted VerValen and Aaron Katzman, both of whom seem to have learned a bit about Chinese cooking along the way.

I am grateful for all the hard work that Drew Gillaspie has put in, researching the text, developing and testing every recipe, and managing the project. Drew also coordinated our studio kitchen crew with great skill, making the production of the shows seem so flawless. My special thanks must also go to Stephanie Liu Jan, my most able assistant, who has so often contributed above and beyond the call of duty. From location scouting to production planning, from guests scheduling to snapping many of the beautiful pictures that appear in this book, Stephanie is the string that binds every element in this project.

The TV series was produced in Toronto at the facilities of FoodNetwork Canada. Special thanks go to Karen Gelbart and Heather Ryall of FoodNetwork for all their support. Behind the scenes we were privileged to have an incomparable staff. In particular, Anne-Sophie Brieger, our Producer, put in long hard hours. She is the best. Director Dennis Saunders and Editor Chris Wenman were as good as they come. But the numerous members of our remote crews, our studio crew, our kitchen staff, and our production office were just as good and just as important. Thanks everyone!

Last but not least, I want to thank my wonderful partners in crime, Geof Drummond and Nat Katzman of A La Carte Communications. Geof Drummond was there at the start when we decided that quick and easy cooking would be an exciting concept. And Nat Katzman, our Executive Producer, has spent more than two years planning, negotiating, creating, and watching over fifty-two TV shows and this book.

It wasn't quick. It wasn't easy. But I hope you agree it was worth it.

Chef Martin Yan
San Mateo, California

CONTENTS

INTRODUCTION

Some people say, "Life is a banquet." For me, that has been quite literally true! Over the years, I've eaten my way across Asia more times than I can count, and I've collected thousands of recipes along the way. It has been a lifelong honor and pleasure to share those recipes with you through my cooking shows and cookbooks.

Some were classic dishes that I discovered in the kitchens of royal palaces. Others were wonderful home recipes passed down from one generation to the next. Master chefs from restaurants all over the world have also shared their culinary secrets with me. And whenever I review this mind-bogglingly enormous collection of recipes, I'm reminded of something that I have known ever since I started cooking as a little kid: with the right approach, almost all Asian dishes, from elaborate banquet creations to everyday, simple one-dish meals, can be made quickly and easily.

Now, I know what you are thinking: "Quick and easy might work for an afternoon snack. But I have guests coming for dinner in two hours. How quick and easy can that be?" The answer comes down to a single word: *preparation*. When you are prepared, any recipe, no matter how complicated it may seem, can be "deconstructed" to fit your timetable. I feel so confident about this that I decided to write a book and do a TV series to show you that you really can prepare quick and easy Asian recipes at home.

When I was growing up in Guangzhou, China, things were very different. Back then, life was slower. My mother had all the time in the world to shop and prepare our daily meals. Sometimes she went to the markets twice a day just to pick up the freshest ingredients at the lowest price; the second time she would bargain with the vendors just when they were closing up their stalls.

Today, life is about two-income families and coordinating schedules. It's about Little League, ballet classes, Scout meetings, having your morning coffee in the car, and eating lunch at your desk. It takes the skill—and sometimes the sense of humor—of a juggler just to gather the entire family for the evening meal. And that meal usually needs to be on the table just minutes after the parent (a.k.a. head chef) has emerged from another grueling rush-hour commute. My own family has experienced all this firsthand. And that's what makes me so excited about quick and easy cooking.

Modern living demands new adjustments. Walk down the aisles of your local supermarket and you'll find countless items designed to speed up the preparation of a home-cooked meal. I remember hearing skeptical snickering about those bags of ready-packed salad greens just a few years ago. How much time could they really save? Two minutes? Five? Well, nobody is laughing now. Consumers are voting with their pocketbooks and tossing those bags of greens into their shopping carts by the millions.

Actually, convenience and time-saving practices have been a big part of Asian cooking for a long time. If you've ever shopped at an Asian grocery store, you know how overwhelming those endless aisles of exotic looking cans, jars, and dehydrated products can be. But once you have familiarized yourself with those strange labels, the jars of sauces and ready-packaged ingredients will become your best time-saving allies in the kitchen. To be fair, up to now, many Asian cookbooks seem to follow the traditional approach in making everything from scratch. Believe me, I have no problem with that. In fact, I highly recommend it if—and it's a big if—you have a lot of time and the full array of cookware and utensils. But today, recipes that call for shortcuts are what most of us need, most of the time.

Even die-hard fans of Asian cooking are sometimes dismayed by the amount of time needed to prepare some Asian dishes. Three minutes of stir-frying might be preceded by hours of shopping and prepping. And many enthusiasts still feel that they need to bring a translator to the Asian grocery store. The truth is, the task of assembling all the right ingredients to make a particular sauce for a dish can be a daunting one. So I say, why reinvent the wheel? Why not make it easier for everybody? In this book, whenever appropriate without sacrificing quality, my recipes use premade ingredients and sauces instead of telling you to do everything from scratch. This will mean less prepping and cooking time, and more time to enjoy your culinary creations with friends and family.

Another shortcut is your friendly Asian deli. As wonderful a cook as my mother is, when an unexpected guest turned up for dinner, she would not hesitate for a second before sending me to the neighborhood deli for barbecued pork or roast duck to round out the dinner menu.

Fortunately, shopping for Asian ingredients is easier than ever these days. For the past few decades, more and more Asian ingredients have been making their way to mainstream supermarkets. I still remember the first time I found fresh bean sprouts in a chain grocery store in the middle of Texas. To me it was quite an emotional experience. Fresh Asian produce, the key to a fresh and healthful Asian meal, has been appearing in produce departments all over the world. On an average day, I can find fresh ginger, napa cabbage, garlic chives, bok choy, tofu, and, of course, bean sprouts in almost any good grocery store. Often, I can even find several brands and textures of fresh tofu. When I first started teaching Chinese cooking many years ago, it wasn't always easy to find a bottle of naturally fermented soy sauce on the market shelf. Today, Asian ingredients are as close as your favorite supermarket.

I am often asked why there has been such an explosion of Asian cuisines, and the answer is simple: Asian cooking, with its emphasis on fresh, healthful ingredients, fits perfectly into today's lifestyles. Actually, the healthful part of the equation may owe as much to picky Asian palates as it does to the lack of complicated food preservation equipment. When my mother went to the food market twice a day, she did it in order to catch the winter melons that had just been unloaded. There weren't too many food wholesalers back in those days, and there sure weren't any refrigerated trucks that could keep the produce fresh. And once the food was brought home, few people had the refrigeration that could protect it from the heat and invading flies. The obvious solution was to cook what you brought home from the market that day. So you see, the emphasis on fresh ingredients was also born out of necessity.

Even though we no longer need to shop every day to ensure quality and freshness, that doesn't mean that the focus on freshness should be compromised. Why? The answer is simple: taste and health. Fresher ingredients make better-tasting dishes that are also better for you. Trust me, once you have tasted truly fresh food, there's no going back. Freshness is addictive—and good for you.

Cooking equipment has changed a lot, too. Today's sophisticated cooks love to have cabinets full of specialized cooking gear. But back in my mother's four-by-five-foot kitchen in Guangzhou, we had a fourteen-inch cast-iron wok and two clay pots. My mother could turn out all kinds of fabulous dishes working with only the most basic kitchen tools. Remember the saying that necessity is the mother of invention? In the Yan family kitchen, my mother was the all-knowing inventor. She taught me very early that a simple wok is much more than just a pan for stir-frying. You can use it to steam, smoke, braise, deep-fry, and more. With my mother's and many others' inventive spirits in mind, this book provides a section describing the basic equipment that you need in the kitchen, along with practical substitutes for items you don't have.

My most recent trips to Asia have given me a chance to savor the dishes from a variety of interesting places. In addition to their colorful history, culture, and heritage, each country has a rich and diverse cuisine and fascinating cooking techniques, and you'll find a number of Taiwanese- and Vietnamese-inspired dishes on these pages, along with many Cantonese, Sichuan, and other Chinese plates. Of course, in keeping with the approach of this volume, these wonderful recipes have been given Martin's quick and easy makeover.

I hope this book adds many happy courses to the banquet of your life, and that you enjoy these quick and easy Asian recipes as much as I did when we tested them in my own family kitchen. And remember, no one but you needs to know just how easy they are. When your friends and family express their delight and amazement that you've created something so wonderful, just do what my mother always does: smile and say, "Enough talking, pass me your bowl!"

QUICK & EASY
TOOLS & TECHNIQUES

People are always asking me for the ultimate cooking tip. The way I see it, tips are so small, but so mighty. So why have just one tip when you can have ten?

Martin Yan's Top Ten Tips for Quick and Easy Asian Cooking

1. **Be sharp:** Have a sharp knife, a sharp mind, and a steady cutting board.
2. **Get fresh:** Use only the freshest ingredients.
3. **Keep it hot:** A hot pan is a good pan.
4. **Be prepared:** Plan and prep ahead.
5. **Keep it uniform:** Cut everything about the same size.
6. **Marinate:** For meat and seafood, marinating is a must!
7. **Think saucy:** A good sauce is the base of any dish.
8. **Be quick:** Once you start, keep it moving.
9. **Be bold:** Experiment and try new flavors and techniques.
10. **Keep smiling:** Relax. It's only dinner. Have fun!

Don't worry, a slight detour from one of these tips won't ruin your dinner or your reputation. These tips are easy reminders that I keep in my head, and over the years, they have served me well. But remember, tips alone won't make the meal for you. For that you will need some basic tools.

Let's start with a sturdy chef's knife and a variety of pots and pans (don't forget the lids!). You will also want to have a box grater, helpful for grating ginger; a nonstick grill pan; a few measuring cups and spoons; a blender or food processor; and last, but not least, lots of zippered plastic bags and resealable plastic containers.

You have all these? Well, great. Now let me give it my quick and easy Asian twist by adding the following items—you may already have some of them—to your shelves.

Chinese cleaver and paring knife: These two hardworking knives are invaluable. Use the cleaver for large items and the paring knife for small tasks and more detailed work.

Wok or stir-fry pan: I recommend the common nonstick 12- or 14-inch woks or nonstick stir-fry pans that are now widely available. You will use less oil when stir-frying than if you used a frying pan, and the high sides help concentrate the heat and keep ingredients from

tumbling over the rim. If you can't find a wok or stir-fry pan, a large nonstick frying pan will also work.

Bamboo steamer: I have so many of these I could stack them up and climb to my second-story window. Steamers come in a variety of sizes, with the most common being 10 or 12 inches, but they come in only one shape—round! Make sure the steamer that you buy fits inside the rim of your wok or stir-fry pan, because that's where you will place it when you steam food. Get one lid for every two or three baskets; the steamers are stackable, so you will only need one lid on top. Steaming is a wonderful way to cook low-fat dishes and to reheat leftovers. If bamboo steamers are unavailable in your area, look for a circular wire rack that has 2- to 3-inch legs. Place a heatproof dish on top of the rack, cover, and steam. Or, improvise with an empty 8-ounce can with both ends removed, placing the dish of food to be steamed on the metal cylinder.

Electric rice cooker: Nearly every Asian kitchen has one of these. Even my mom, the traditional home cook, has a rice cooker. More than a perfect cooker for rice, this gadget can make a variety of one-dish meals and even soup. The best part is that it does all the work for you. You put in the ingredients, walk away, and when the rice is ready, it will let you know. I am hoping that an inventor will come out with one that can page me when my rice is done. Meanwhile, you should pick out a size that's right for your family. In general they come in 6-, 8-, or 10-cup sizes. Look for one with a nonstick interior for easy cleanup. Make sure to read the manufacturer's instructions, as each rice cooker is a bit different and cooking times can vary. Some even have a "keep warm" button that will keep cooked rice warm and ready to eat for hours.

Deep-frying thermometer: This lets you know when your oil is at the perfect temperature for cooking. If you don't have one, you can test the oil with a small piece of what you are deep-frying. When slipped into the oil, it should be quickly surrounded by bubbles.

Now, for the extras, the tools that are not must-haves, but that definitely make cooking Asian dishes a lot more fun and a lot easier.

Chinese skimmer: Think of the skimmer as your third hand in the pan. Use it to remove items from boiling water or hot oil. This bamboo-handled brass-mesh basket comes in a wide assortment of sizes. It is like a supersized slotted spoon, and once you try one out, you'll want to use it in all your cooking, not just your Asian dishes.

Cooking chopsticks: These are longer and larger than the chopsticks you get with Chinese takeout. Usually 12 to 16 inches long, these wooden chopsticks are great for turning food in hot water or oil.

Juicer: Who doesn't like freshly squeezed juices? But think outside the orange-juice box. How about lemon or lime? With a press-style manual juicer—not a typical Asian gadget, but very handy nonetheless—you will get every last drop of juice from citrus fruit, and you get a nice little workout in the process.

Microplane grater: A relatively new invention and also one of my favorite contemporary gadgets. For grating ginger or zesting citrus, this grater is, well, simply the greatest!

Slicer: This handy tool comes in a variety of styles. You can find inexpensive plastic slicing contraptions with metal blades that make an array of different cuts, so you can slice or julienne a whole pile of veggies in just a few seconds.

QUICK & EASY ASIAN TECHNIQUES

Most Western home cooks are well acquainted with all the basic cooking methods: baking, grilling (indoors and out), boiling, sautéing, panfrying, and searing. Here are a few techniques unique to Asian cooking that deserve some extra attention.

Marinating: A must when you are preparing most Asian meat, poultry, and seafood dishes. Marination not only enhances flavor, but also helps to seal in moisture. For a better result, let the meat and marinade stand for a few minutes before cooking. Notice that I said a few minutes. Western marinating can take hours, while Asian marinating is quick and easy.

Stir-frying: It's not rocket science, but there are a few tricks of the trade that are worth noting. The number eight is a lucky number in Chinese culture. Since some of you are beginners, here are my eight tips for stir-frying to bring you good luck:

1. **Cut** the meat and seafood into bite-sized pieces before marinating.
2. **Chop** all your vegetables to bite-sized pieces.
3. **Arrange** vegetables in the order they are cooked.
4. **Mix** your sauce ingredients before you start cooking. This allows you to give your undivided attention to the dish you are stir-frying.
5. **Preheat** your wok or pan. Do not add the oil or other ingredients to the pan until it is hot.
6. **"Season" the oil.** Many recipes call for the garlic, ginger, shallot, or chili to go into the pan first, to flavor the oil for the cooking that follows.

7. **Avoid overcrowding.** Most recipes call for less than a pound of meat. A crowded pan makes even cooking of all the ingredients difficult.

8. **Keep it moving.** Remember, it's stir-frying, so stir, *don't* stare!

Steaming: A steam bath is good for your health and your food! What's more, it's quick and easy once you know how. Simply add a few inches of water (see page 14 for how to improvise a steamer) to a wok or other deep pan. Place a bamboo steamer basket inside the rim of the pan or a wire rack on the bottom and bring the water to a boil. Place the dish you are steaming inside the steamer or on top of the rack. Cover the basket or the pan and steam according to the recipe's recommended time. If you are steaming for a longer period, be sure to recheck the water level periodically. Be aware that steam can burn you, so use caution when removing lids and dishes.

Frying: We are living in a time when oil is too often looked upon with suspicion. Don't be afraid to use oil in your cooking. When used properly, it seals in the moisture and juice of the ingredients better than most other cooking techniques. Also, not all frying uses a lot of oil. Even deep-frying, if done at the proper temperature (usually around 350°F on a deep-frying thermometer), can produce light, crisp results without an excess of oil. Just remember to drain the food when it comes out of the pan. For deep-frying, you will need only enough oil for the ingredient to be fully submerged, so that it can move freely during cooking. For shallow-frying, the ingredient is only partially submerged in oil, with the amount of oil dependent on the size of the pan.

Want more? Here are a few other quick and easy techniques that are great additions to your repertoire of cooking skills:

Segmenting citrus: Don't worry, this is easier than it looks. Simply slice the ends off the fruit with a knife, hold the fruit with one cut side on the board, and slice downward from top to bottom to remove the peel in strips, working your way around the fruit. Cut deeply enough to remove the white pith. Now cut toward the center of the fruit on one side of the membrane. Slice the fruit segment while leaving the membrane intact.

Rehydrating: Yes, this is a technique. Dried black mushrooms are common ingredients in quick Asian dishes, and they must be reconstituted before using. Place the dried ingredient in warm water to cover until softened. It can be as quick as 5 minutes or as long as 15 minutes. Drain the liquid, and the ingredient is ready to use.

Roll-cutting: Common for cutting long, cylindrical vegetables such as eggplants or carrots. Simply cut the end of the vegetable off at a diagonal, give the vegetable a quarter turn, and slice straight down. Keep rolling and cutting until you reach the end.

Zesting: When a recipe calls for lemon zest, don't panic! Pick up the zester and let the lemon have it! A Microplane grater or a box grater can also be used for zesting. Don't grate too hard, as you want to avoid the white pith, which can add a bitter taste. Also, zest the fruit before you juice it.

Toasting nuts: No, I'm not talking about people who raise their glasses every 30 seconds and yell *"kung pei!"* What I am talking about is placing a heavy frying pan over medium-high heat and adding the nuts to the hot surface for toasting. This brings out the flavor and aroma of the nuts' rich oils, making them even tastier for any dish in which you use them. Once you smell the fragrance and see that the nuts are beginning to brown, remove them from the pan. Or, place the nuts in a baking pan and bake in a 325°F oven for 6 to 10 minutes (the timing depends on the nut). Set a timer and watch them carefully. Nuts can go from toasted to burned in a matter of seconds.

Now you have the basic tools at hand and a general understanding of the quick and easy Asian cooking techniques. Your next task is to learn what is in the Asian pantry and how to make a few basic recipes.

QUICK & EASY BASICS

STOCKING UP

A well-stocked pantry and refrigerator are important to quick and easy Asian cooking. They allow even the busiest cook to prepare a meal in a minimal amount of time with only a short trip to the grocery store to purchase highly perishable or specialty items. If necessary, visit your local Asian market to buy the staples. Adjust your shopping list to reflect your preferences.

PANTRY ITEMS
These are nonrefrigerated items found on market shelves. They are divided into several categories.

BARE BASICS: You probably already have many of these staples on hand, as they are used in a variety of cuisines.

Brown sugar	Honey
Cayenne pepper	Peanut butter
Cornstarch	Red chili flakes
Flour	White pepper

SAUCES: These premade sauces add dimension to many Asian dishes. You'll be able to find most of them on your supermarket shelves in the Asian section. Store them in the refrigerator after opening.

Black bean garlic sauce	Plum sauce
Chili garlic sauce	Soy sauce, regular and dark
Fish sauce	Sweet-and-sour sauce
Hoisin sauce	Teriyaki sauce
Oyster-flavored sauce	

RICE AND NOODLES: Dried and shelf stable, these staples will last for months and provide the base for a quick and easy meal.

Long-grain rice	Soba or somen noodles
Rice stick noodles	

OILS, VINEGARS, AND WINE

Chinese black vinegar or balsamic
  vinegar
Chinese rice wine or dry sherry
Mirin

Rice vinegar, unseasoned
Sesame oil
Vegetable oil

CANNED GOODS

Baby corn
Bamboo shoots
Broth, chicken, beef, and vegetable
Pineapple chunks

Straw mushrooms
Unsweetened coconut milk
Water chestnuts

NUTS, SEEDS, AND DRIED FRUITS: Nuts have a high oil content, so store them in the freezer to extend their shelf life.

Cashews
Cranberries
Glazed walnuts
Peanuts

Pine nuts
Sesame seeds
Walnuts

SEASONINGS AND MISCELLANEOUS ITEMS

Chinese five-spice powder
Chinese mustard
Curry powder
Dried black mushrooms

Panko
Star anise
Thai curry paste, yellow and green
Wasabi powder or paste

REFRIGERATOR AND FREEZER ITEMS

These items range from vegetables to tofu. Although the refrigerated items are perishable, many of them will last a few weeks if stored properly. Check expiration dates on tofu if you are not using immediately. Also, fresh wrappers and noodles can be divided into small packages and frozen for later use. I keep a variety of sizes of zippered freezer bags on hand. They prove useful after a big trip to the grocery store.

REFRIGERATOR ITEMS

VEGETABLES, FRUITS, AND SEASONINGS

Cilantro (Wash to remove any dirt, wrap loosely in a paper towel, and put into a zippered plastic bag. I've had cilantro remain fresh after 10 days.)

Garlic (To save time, purchase already peeled garlic.)

Ginger (Peel the nub of ginger, slice or chop, and store in oil or Chinese rice wine in the refrigerator.)

Green onions (Wash and trim off the roots, leave whole or cut into 1- to 2-inch pieces, wrap in a damp paper towel, and put into a zippered plastic bag. Remember to use the white and green portions unless otherwise specified in the recipe.)

Lemongrass (Cut or chop a bunch and store in the freezer for later use. It will retain most of the flavor nuances.)

Lemons

Limes

Onions, yellow or white

NOODLES, WRAPPERS, AND TOFU

Dumpling wrappers

Fresh Chinese egg noodles

Tofu, firm or soft

MISCELLANEOUS

Chinese sausage

Miso

FREEZER ITEMS

FISH AND POULTRY

Chicken breast or thigh

Raw shrimp, peeled and deveined

Salmon or other fish fillets

VEGETABLES

Corn

Edamame

MISCELLANEOUS

Ice cream

Premade dumplings

ONLINE SOURCES

If you don't have an Asian market close by, you can get everything you need to stock your quick and easy pantry on the Internet. Here are a few companies that offer a nice selection of Asian ingredients.

MELISSA'S WORLD VARIETY PRODUCE

The source for Asian produce and such specialty items as crystallized ginger and dried mushrooms. You'll find excellent descriptions and pictures of even the most exotic vegetables and tips on how to prepare them. The site carries a wide selection of vegetables and fruits from all cuisines.

www.melissas.com

IMPORT FOOD

Specializing in Thai ingredients, Import Food sells the hard-to-find fresh kaffir lime leaves. Keep in mind that these delicate leaves are seasonal, organically grown in California, and vary in size from summer to winter, but are still great quality year-round. You'll get a large amount, so give them to friends or freeze for later use.

www.importfood.com

ETHNIC GROCER

The online resource for anything ethnic. You can find almost any nonperishable Asian ingredient and have it delivered to your doorstep.

www.ethnicgrocer.com

EARTHLY DELIGHTS

An excellent resource for any gourmet chef or food lover. It offers a wide variety of exotic and gourmet products from all styles of cuisines and a nice selection of Asian seasonings.

www.earthlydelights.com

PACIFIC RIM GOURMET

Offers entire pantries with one click of your mouse.

www.pacificgourmet.com

ORIENTAL GROCERY

In the Stocking Up section, I recommend that you have Chinese sausage on hand. Since it is only available in Chinese markets, and there is no substitute, I've found an online source.

www.orientalgrocery.com

GLOSSARY OF INGREDIENTS

Baby Corn Young, pale yellow, tiny ears of corn that are sweet and crunchy. They are found in most supermarkets, canned or refrigerated packed in water. If adding the canned to a delicate soup, blanch in boiling water for 1 minute before using to remove the slight tinny flavor. Use this versatile vegetable in stir-fries, braised dishes, salads, and soups.

Bamboo Shoots Tender and crisp, bamboo shoots have a naturally sweet taste. They are sold canned, refrigerated packed in water, and vacuum-packed in a variety of forms: sliced, shredded, or even whole. Bamboo shoots can be used in almost any dish to add texture.

Basil If possible, use Thai basil, which looks similar to regular basil, but has darker green leaves and a purplish stem. The pungent, slightly mint flavor enhances many Asian dishes. Regular basil can be substituted. Store lightly wrapped in a damp paper towel in a zippered plastic bag in the refrigerator.

Bean Sprouts Also known as mung bean sprouts. Most markets sell 1-pound bags of these mild, crunchy sprouts. Purchase them only when you are planning to use them, as they are highly perishable. Storing them immersed in fresh water can extend their shelf life slightly. Bean sprouts can be eaten raw or cooked.

Bean Thread Noodles Also called glass noodles or cellophane noodles, these semitransparent dried noodles, made from mung bean starch, are sold in large or one-portion bundles. Typically the noodles are softened in warm water until pliable, then added to a dish; when cooked, they absorb the flavoring of the broth or sauce. Use them in stir-fries, braised dishes, or soups.

Black Bean Garlic Sauce Made from salted black beans, garlic, and rice wine; some brands also contain dried chilies. An intensely flavored sauce, it should be used in small amounts and is best when cooked. Store in the refrigerator after opening.

Black Pepper Sauce A prepared sauce found in Asian markets. Used primarily in stir-fries. Store in the refrigerator after opening.

Chili Garlic Sauce Made from a blend of fresh and dried chilies and vinegar, it can also contain garlic, ginger, soybeans, and sesame oil. Store in the refrigerator after opening.

Chinese Black Vinegar Made by fermenting a mixture of rice, wheat, and either millet or sorghum. It possesses a sweet, smoky flavor and is used in cooking and as a condiment. Balsamic vinegar may be substituted.

Chinese Chives Long, thin, and flat, Chinese chives, which resemble long blades of grass, add a slightly garlicky, oniony flavor to dumpling fillings, soups, and stir-fries.

Chinese Egg Noodles Sold both fresh and dried, these noodles, made from wheat flour, eggs, and water, come in a variety of thicknesses. If you cannot locate Chinese noodles, substitute a similar thickness from the Italian pasta family and keep on cooking.

Chinese Five-Spice Powder A cocoa-colored powder composed of ground cinnamon, star anise, cloves, fennel, and Sichuan peppercorns, it adds a slightly spicy, yet sweet flavor to braised meats, roasts, and barbecues. Use sparingly, as this pungent spice can overpower any dish.

Chinese Long Beans Part of the black-eyed pea family, long beans are drier and denser than green beans. Also known as yard-long beans, they have a mild flavor and crisp texture that make them ideal for pungent and spicy seasonings. As with most vegetables, be careful not to overcook, as they will become unpleasantly mushy.

Chinese Mustard Made from a mixture of dry mustard powder and liquid, this pungent and spicy condiment delivers a clean-tasting hotness. It is used as a dipping sauce for Chinese appetizers and is added to sauces, dressings, and marinades. Store in the refrigerator after opening.

Chinese Rice Wine Known also as Shaoxing wine, this richly flavored, amber liquid is made from fermented glutinous rice and millet and is typically aged between 10 and 100 years. Most grocery-store shelves carry rice wines that are good for cooking, rather than drinking. Dry sherry can be substituted.

Chinese Sausage Mildly sweet links made from pork and pork fat, duck, or beef. They are 4 to 6 inches long, a deep red to brown, and are usually seasoned with salt, sugar, and rice wine and then cured, giving them a bumpy texture. Used in an assortment of preparations, including stir-fries, braises, and steamed dishes, they are found in vacuum-sealed packages on the shelves of Asian markets. Keep in mind they must be cooked before eating. Store in the refrigerator after opening; they will keep for up to 1 month.

Cilantro Also known as Chinese parsley or fresh coriander, this indispensable herb has flat, ruffled leaves with a distinct aromatic flavor. Store wrapped in a damp paper towel in a zippered plastic bag in the refrigerator.

Crystallized Ginger Fresh ginger that is first slowly cooked in sugared water and then rolled in granulated sugar, resulting in a mellow, but spicy-sweet taste. It can be added to savory and sweet dishes to provide complex flavor.

Curry Paste Classified by their color—green, yellow, and red—these Thai pastes are a blend of a number of fresh herbs and spices that yield an intense, thick, moist mixture. They are found premade in jars, cans, and other types of containers on most supermarket shelves. Cook the paste in oil or a small amount of liquid to allow the flavors to bloom before adding other ingredients. Store in the refrigerator after opening.

Curry Powder Mild to hot, aromatic yellow powder made up of a blend of six or more spices, usually including cardamom, cinnamon, cumin, cloves, black peppercorns, and turmeric. Try both domestic and imported brands to find your favorite.

Daikon Japanese radish usually 8 to 14 inches long and 2 to 3 inches in diameter. Peel this crisp, white, peppery radish before eating. Eat raw or pickled, or add to stews and stir-fries.

Dashi Japanese soup base made from a blend of dried bonito (a type of tuna), *konbu* (sea kelp), and other ingredients. Usually sold in bouillon cubes, in granules, or in liquid form.

Dried Black Mushrooms Also known as shiitake or Chinese mushrooms, dried black mushrooms have brownish black caps with a tan underside; a rich, meaty texture; and a robust, wild mushroom flavor. Rehydrate (see page 16) and discard the woody stems before adding to anything from soups to stir-fries.

Dumpling Wrappers Made from wheat flour, water, and egg, wrappers are sold round or square in a variety of thicknesses. They can be used to wrap fillings for potstickers, wontons, and steamed dumplings, or they can be sliced and fried for a snack or garnish. Stocked in the refrigerated section of most supermarkets, wrappers freeze well.

Edamame Fresh, sweet, young soybeans sold shelled and in the pod, both fresh and frozen. This fiber-rich vegetable is a great addition to soups and fried rice, or makes a good appetizer served in the pod. Follow package instructions for cooking times, as they vary from brand to brand.

Eggplant Chinese eggplant is white to lavender, and Japanese is light purple to purple-black. Both are long and slender and used as you would a globe eggplant: baked, fried, grilled, braised, steamed, and in stir-fries. The two can be used interchangeably and are relatively sweet. Unlike globe varieties, they do not typically need to be salted or peeled.

Enoki Mushrooms Tiny white mushrooms with small caps and slender stems 2 to 3 inches long. They have a mild flavor and are often added to clear soups or used raw in salads or as an elegant garnish. You will find them vacuum-packed in small packages in the produce section.

Fish Sauce An all-purpose amber-colored, salty flavoring agent made by pressing out the liquid from fermented anchovy-like fish. It is used to season dishes as they cook and as a table condiment, and is as common in Southeast Asia as soy sauce is in China. Once you open the bottle, the fish sauce will become more pungent with age. Store in the refrigerator if you do not use it often.

Furikake A seaweed-based Japanese seasoning mixture with no single recipe. Some brands include sesame seeds and sugar, while others feature cayenne pepper, bonito flakes, and dried egg. Sprinkle it on tofu, vegetables, or even a plain bowl of steamed rice. An excellent condiment to have on hand, it is carried in specialty stores and Asian markets.

Gai Lan Also known as Chinese broccoli (*gai lan* is the Cantonese name), this dark green vegetable with round stems and relatively broad leaves is used in soups or stir-fries, or is served simply steamed or boiled. Peel the thick stems to shorten the cooking time.

Hoisin Sauce This dark reddish brown sauce is a combination of fermented soybeans, vinegar, garlic, sugar, and spices. It has a sweet, tangy flavor and is often used to make barbecue marinades, to glaze meats, and as a condiment for such popular dishes as *mu shu* pork and Peking duck. Store in the refrigerator after opening.

Jicama A crunchy vegetable with a mild flavor that marries well with almost any food, jicama can be steamed, braised, deep-fried, or used in soups, salads, or stir-fries. It makes a good substitute for water chestnuts and vice versa. Store in the refrigerator and peel before use.

Kaffir Lime Leaves A Southeast Asian herb, which is quite difficult to find in most grocery stores, but is available through the Internet (see page 22). Thinly shred the bright green leaves and add them to any dish for a delicate lemon-lime flavor. Lime zest can be used in their place, but, unlike the lime leaves, it should be added at the end of the cooking process, as it turns bitter the longer it cooks.

Kimchee Spicy, pickled cabbage of Korean origin. Widely sold in jars, in hot and mild styles, in the Asian produce section of many supermarkets, kimchee is a great accompaniment to soups and rice dishes. Although different in flavor from Sichuan preserved vegetable (page 29), mild kimchee can stand in for the Sichuan vegetable when necessary.

Lemongrass A fragrant herb with a delicate, lemony flavor, lemongrass resembles a woody stalk with coarse leaves. To prepare, remove the outer tough layer of leaves and discard, then use only the bottom 4 inches or so of the stalk. Once chopped, it can be stored in the freezer for up to a month.

Lotus Root A sausage-shaped vegetable that is sold linked. To use, peel and slice crosswise, revealing a cross section of lacy holes that run the length of the vegetable. With a mild, almost nutty flavor, it can be used in soups and stir-fries to add texture, or it can be thinly sliced and deep-fried for garnish or chips.

Mint Fresh mint is added to give a cool, refreshing flavor to dishes. Store it wrapped in a damp paper towel in a zippered plastic bag in the refrigerator.

Mirin Made from glutinous rice, this Japanese sweet cooking wine adds rich flavor and a glossy sheen to dishes.

Miso A paste of Japanese origin made from crushed fermented soybeans and barley, rice, or wheat. It comes in different colors, but only white miso is used in this book. It is rich in protein and is often used to make soups, sauces, marinades, and salad dressings.

Napa Cabbage Mild in flavor, this versatile cabbage has either short (Chinese) or tall (Japanese) stalks. It has sweet, cream-colored stalks and ruffled, pale green or white leaves. Use in stir-fries, braises, salads, and soups.

Nori Dried seaweed that is pressed into thin sheets. Used primarily in making sushi.

Oyster-Flavored Sauce A thick, dark brown, all-purpose seasoning made from oyster extracts, sugar, and seasonings. It can be used plain for dipping or added to a sauce. Cooking will mellow its intensity. Store in the refrigerator after opening.

Panko Dried, toasted Japanese bread crumbs that give a crunchy coating to deep-fried foods. The crumbs are larger and coarser than regular bread crumbs, and they retain their crisp texture particularly well after frying.

Pickled Ginger Two basic types are available, Chinese ginger and sushi ginger. Chinese ginger is cured in brine and then soaked in a sugar-vinegar solution that turns it red. It is used in everything from stir-fries to soups. Sushi ginger is pickled in salt, sugar, and vinegar with a pink dye, and is usually served alongside sushi or sashimi. Both types can usually be found in the Asian section of the supermarket. If Chinese ginger is unavailable, use sushi ginger in its place.

Plum Sauce This sweet and tangy sauce is traditionally used as a dipping sauce, and is sometimes called duck sauce when served with egg rolls in a neighborhood Chinese restaurant. At its best, it is a perfect balance of sweet, tangy, and salty tastes. Add it to sauces and dressings, or use it plain as a dipping sauce for nearly anything crispy. Store in the refrigerator after opening.

Plum Wine Japanese wine made from plums and alcohol, it is sweet, yet slightly sour, and adds an interesting dimension to sauces. No substitute will replicate the flavor nuances, but a combination of plum sauce and a bit of Chinese rice wine will work in a pinch.

Ponzu Sauce Sauce made from mirin, lemon juice, soy sauce, and sugar that is used as a dip for seafood, as a marinade, or as a sauce. Store in the refrigerator after opening. If you cannot find it at the store, it is easy to make at home (page 36).

Rice Long-grain rice, the most popular rice in China, is the least starchy of all of the rices. Once cooked, the grains are easily separated and have a dry, fluffy look, ideal qualities for fried rice. Jasmine and basmati are two types of long-grain rice. Glutinous rice, also known as sweet or sticky rice, is a type of short-grain rice that has an opaque, milky white look when raw, and a soft, sticky, translucent look when cooked. Short-grain rice is preferred for Japanese and Korean cuisines, and is used for making sushi rice. Medium-grain rice, which is regarded as an all-purpose rice, can be used when short-grain rice is unavailable.

Rice Paper Brittle, semitransparent round or triangular sheets made from rice flour. The sheets are softened in warm water before using as wrappers for a variety of fillings. Served both fresh and deep-fried.

Rice Stick Noodles These dried noodles, made from ground long-grain rice and water, are available in a variety of thicknesses. They are cooked in boiling water until tender, and then used as a bed for a stir-fry in place of rice, or are added to soups or stir-fries.

Rice Vinegar Made from fermented rice, this Japanese product has a milder and sweeter flavor than distilled white vinegar. It is sold both seasoned and unseasoned. The former is noticeably sweet and should not be used in place of the latter. The recipes in this book use unseasoned rice vinegar unless otherwise specified.

Sake This fermented Japanese rice wine comes in thousands of types, which are graded by quality. It is typically used in cooking to give a dish a more complex flavor and sometimes to balance saltiness. As with grape wine, you should cook with sake that is of drinking quality. Once opened, sake should be used quickly or stored in the refrigerator.

Sesame Oil An aromatic, strong-flavored, golden or dark brown oil made from roasted white sesame seeds. It has a distinctive nutty flavor, is primarily used as a flavoring agent, rather than for cooking, and is often added toward the end of cooking. Do not confuse it with the light sesame oils made from unroasted seeds that are usually stocked in natural-foods stores. Store in your pantry, or in the refrigerator to extend its shelf life.

Sesame Seed Paste Ground toasted sesame seeds, primarily used in Asian cuisine. Found on the grocery shelves but should be stored in the refrigerator once opened. Tahini is a good substitution.

Sesame Seeds Both black and white seeds are sold, and both are used to flavor and garnish dishes. Black sesame seeds are slightly bitter, while the white ones have a sweet, nutty flavor. Toast the white seeds unless otherwise specified.

Shallots Usually the size of a walnut, shallots are extremely popular in Southeast Asian dishes. They have a mild flavor and can be thinly sliced for use in stir-fries, or the slices can be deep-fried for use as a garnish.

Shiitake Mushrooms Meaty and rich, these mushrooms are sold fresh and dried. Remove the stems from fresh mushrooms, as they are too tough to eat. The caps can be sliced and added to salads, stir-fries, or soups. Store mushrooms in the refrigerator in a paper bag. For directions on using dried shiitakes, *see* Dried Black Mushrooms.

Sichuan Preserved Vegetable Can be any type of vegetable but primarily mustard greens, bok choy, or napa cabbage. It is preserved with salt, vinegar, and spices and is sold vacuum-sealed, canned, or in jars. Store in the refrigerator after opening for up to a month.

Snow Peas Flat, green pods with a sweet, sugary flavor. Cook briefly to retain the crisp, texture, or use raw in salads. Remove the ends and the strings that run along the sides.

Soba Noodles Brownish gray Japanese noodles made from buckwheat flour and wheat flour. They are chewy and have a nutty flavor. Typically found dried, you might be lucky enough to locate them fresh in an Asian market. Good in soups, stir-fries, or served chilled.

Somen Noodles Delicate, white, thin noodles made from wheat flour with a bit of oil and sold dried in most supermarkets. They can be cooked and served chilled as a salad or with a dipping sauce, stir-fried with vegetables, or added to a soup.

Soy Nuts Toasted and seasoned soybeans used as a garnish or eaten as a snack.

Soy Sauce Made from naturally fermented soybeans and a grain, usually wheat, soy sauces come in a few different types. The two most common products are regular soy sauce, which is used in cooking and as a table condiment, and dark soy sauce, which is a mixture of regular soy sauce and molasses. The latter, used for cooking but not typically at the table, is much thicker and delivers a sweet, full-bodied flavor. If you do not use soy sauce regularly, store it in the refrigerator, as it will continue to ferment when open or left at room temperature.

Spring Roll Wrappers Made from a batter of wheat flour and water, these thin, pliable sheets are wrapped around savory fillings and deep-fried, producing a light and flaky result. Do not confuse these batter-made wrappers with egg roll wrappers, which are made from a dough. Store in the refrigerator or freezer.

Star Anise This aromatic spice looks like a star, and each point encloses a shiny, mahogany brown seed. It adds a distinct licorice flavor to stews, braises, and marinades. Avoid eating the pod, as it is very hard and you might crack a tooth. Do not worry if the star anise is broken; simply count out eight points, or "rays," to equal a single whole spice.

Straw Mushrooms Found only canned, these small mushrooms have a firm texture and delicate flavor. Before using them in any dish, it is best to blanch them in boiling water for 1 minute to remove the tinny flavor that results from canning. Asian markets carry both peeled and unpeeled straw mushrooms; use either one.

Sugar Snap Peas These thick, bright green edible pods conceal tiny peas. They have a sweet, sugary flavor and crisp, crunchy texture, making them perfect for eating raw with a dip or for adding to soups or stir-fries. Most sugar snap peas have no fibrous strings, which means they require no preparation other than a good rinsing.

Sweet Chili Sauce Made from ground red chilies, sugar, garlic, and salt, this thick sauce is a wonderful combination of sweet, spicy, and tangy flavors. It is traditionally used as a dipping sauce, but can also be used as a glaze, or it can be added to other sauces to deliver a spicy punch to a dish. Store in the refrigerator after opening.

Tahini Traditional Middle Eastern paste made from ground unroasted white sesame seeds. It is a widely available option to Chinese sesame seed paste, which is made from ground toasted white sesame seeds. If you can't find either paste, substitute peanut butter.

Taro Root This dense tuber, which has a rough, brown skin and pale (sometimes purplish), speckled flesh, turns starchy and has a sweet, nutty flavor when cooked. You'll find large and small taro roots, and they can be used interchangeably in this book. Never attempt to eat taro raw, as it is inedible. If you cannot find taro, use a starchy potato in its place. Store in a cool, dark place.

Tofu A high-protein food made from cooked soybeans and water, tofu is sold in a variety of textures. Soft or silken tofu is known for its smooth, light texture. Because it breaks apart easily during cooking, it is best steamed and served drizzled with a light sauce or cut into small cubes for a soup. Regular or firm tofu is denser and has a spongy interior; it is great for stir-fries or braises and is often deep-fried, forming an airy puff. Pressed tofu is a hard, flat compressed block; it is sold plain and in a variety of flavors, including teriyaki. Check the expiration date on every tofu package before purchase, and then store in the refrigerator. Store leftover tofu immersed in water.

Turmeric Bitter, pungent spice with an intense rust color that stains anything with which it comes in contact. Related to ginger, turmeric, which botanically is a rhizome, is sometimes available fresh in markets. Ground turmeric is more common, however. It is used in sauces, curries, and other dishes, adding a bright, deep yellow color. For the best flavor, toast the turmeric lightly in a dry frying pan to release the aroma and temper the bitterness.

Unsweetened Coconut Milk The unsweetened liquid extracted from freshly grated coconut. Typically used in curries and soups, and most commonly sold canned, coconut milk adds flavor and creaminess to dishes.

Vegetable Oil Any type of oil obtained from plants. Use a pure oil (rather than a blend of oils) with a high smoking point, such as canola, corn, peanut, or soybean.

Wasabi A Japanese root with a sharp, fiery flavor that is similar in character to Western horseradish but is unrelated. Available in powdered form, which is mixed with water to form a paste, and also sold as a paste in tubes. Both types are found in Asian stores and in some supermarkets. Store the paste in the refrigerator after opening and the powder in a tightly sealed container in the pantry.

Water Chestnuts Sold fresh in season, still enclosed in their shiny brown skins, in the produce aisle, or year-round peeled and whole or sliced and packed in water in cans in the produce aisle or Asian foods section. Fresh water chestnuts have a slightly sweet, starchy flesh, while their canned counterparts have a similar texture but are not as sweet. Add water chestnuts to almost any dish for texture. I've even used them in desserts. Store unused water chestnuts covered with water in the refrigerator for up to 1 week.

Wood Ears These are a type of fungus, or mushroom, that grow on trees and are usually found dried in Asian markets. Bland in flavor, they are used primarily for their smooth, slightly chewy texture. They must be rehydrated (see page 16) before using.

BASIC RECIPES

Here are short, simple recipes that are either a quick and easy Asian must or are something that can jazz up a dish with little effort. Most of the dressings, condiments, syrups, and sauces will keep for a few weeks in tightly covered containers in the refrigerator.

STEAMED WHITE RICE

Cooking rice is a skill that anyone can quickly master. Make a large batch and use leftovers in soups, to make fried rice, or in one of the many recipes in this book that call for refrigerated cooked long-grain rice. I am often asked why steamed rice recipes instruct you to rinse the rice. This usually is only necessary if you purchase rice in large quantities. If you purchase only small amounts, 1- to 5-pound plastic bags, there is no need to rinse. This recipe is for stove-top cooking. If you are using a rice cooker, follow the manufacturer's instructions.

MAKES ABOUT 5 ½ CUPS

2 cups long-grain rice

3 cups water

Place the rice in a 3-quart saucepan with a tight-fitting lid. Add the water and bring to a boil over high heat. Cook until craterlike holes form on the surface of the rice, about 6 minutes. Reduce the heat to low, cover, and cook, undisturbed, for 10 minutes. Remove from the heat and let the rice stand, covered, for a few minutes. Remove the cover, fluff the rice with a fork, and serve.

SUSHI RICE

You should make relatively small batches of this rice, as it is best used the day it is prepared. Serve grilled meat or seafood over scoops of the rice, or get adventurous and try your hand at sushi. Use short-grain rice, sometimes sold as "sushi rice," or medium-grain rice for this recipe. Both will produce excellent results.

2 cups short-grain rice

2 cups water

¼ cup rice vinegar

2½ tablespoons sugar

1 tablespoon mirin

¾ teaspoon salt

Place the rice in a bowl. Add cold water to cover and wash the rice well by rubbing it between your hands, then drain. Repeat twice more. Pour the rice into a strainer to drain. Place the rinsed rice and the 2 cups water in a 2- to 3-quart saucepan. Bring to a boil over high heat, reduce the heat to low, cover, and cook for 20 minutes. Turn off the heat and let the rice stand for 10 minutes.

In a small pan, heat the vinegar, sugar, mirin, and salt over medium heat until the sugar dissolves. Remove from the heat.

Turn out the cooked rice into a large wooden or plastic bowl, and pour the vinegar mixture evenly over the rice. Fold the liquid in with a wooden rice paddle. At the same time, fan the rice to bring out the luster of the grains. Continue folding and fanning until the rice absorbs all the liquid. Cover with a damp cloth and let stand until ready to use. It will hold at room temperature for up to 4 hours.

QUICK GLUTINOUS RICE

This short-grain rice, also called sweet or sticky rice, usually requires soaking overnight before cooking, but I've discovered a way to cook delicious glutinous rice in about 30 minutes. If you visit Thailand, you will find similar rice served with your meal and eaten with the fingers. Serve this sticky rice with a main course, or mixed with sweetened coconut milk or syrup for dessert.

2 cups glutinous rice

4 cups water

Place the rice in a large bowl, fill the bowl with cold water, and then drain. Repeat until the water runs clear, then drain into a strainer. In a large saucepan with a tight-fitting lid, bring the 4 cups water to a boil over high

continued

heat. Add the rice and, leaving the heat on high, stir once. When the water returns to a boil, boil uncovered for 2 minutes. Cover, remove from the heat, and let stand for 2 minutes. Using the lid to keep the rice in the pan, drain off the water into the sink. Return the pan to low heat, re-cover, and cook for 25 minutes. Remove from the heat, stir with chopsticks, and keep warm until serving.

QUICK ASIAN CHICKEN BROTH

This flavor-enhanced broth can be used as a base for soups, or you can add cooked noodles and some green vegetables to it for a quick and simple soup.

MAKES ABOUT
3 QUARTS (12 CUPS)

3 quarts (12 cups) chicken broth

2 green onions, cut into 2-inch pieces

4 quarter-sized slices ginger, lightly crushed

2 tablespoons soy sauce

1/8 teaspoon white pepper

1/4 teaspoon salt

In a large pot, combine all the ingredients and bring to a boil over high heat. Reduce the heat to low and simmer, uncovered, for 10 minutes. Use immediately, or let cool, cover, and refrigerate for up to 1 week.

SPICY SOY DIPPING SAUCE

Use this versatile dipping sauce with potstickers, spring rolls, or over plain white rice. Adjust the chili garlic sauce to the level of heat that you prefer.

MAKES ABOUT 3/4 CUP

6 tablespoons soy sauce

1/4 cup Chinese black vinegar or balsamic vinegar

2 teaspoons sesame oil

2 teaspoons chili garlic sauce

In a bowl, combine all the ingredients and stir until combined. Store in a covered container in the refrigerator; it will keep for up to 3 weeks.

SOUTHEAST ASIAN ALL-PURPOSE DIPPING SAUCE

Use this tart, hot, salty sauce as a dip for spring rolls, as a sauce for steamed fish or grilled meats, or with a simple mixture of rice noodles and thinly sliced vegetables.

¼ cup water

¼ cup fish sauce

3 tablespoons fresh lime juice

2 tablespoons rice vinegar

2 tablespoons sugar

1 clove garlic, minced

1 small red chili, seeded and minced, or ½ teaspoon red chili flakes

In a bowl, combine all the ingredients and stir until the sugar dissolves. Store in a covered container in the refrigerator; it will keep for up to 2 weeks.

MAKES ABOUT ¾ CUP

PEANUT DIPPING SAUCE

This rich dipping sauce goes well with fresh rice-paper rolls. You can also use it as a thick dressing for a quick salad, or stir it into hot noodles for an easy lunch.

2 teaspoons vegetable oil

1 clove garlic, minced

⅔ cup chicken broth

¼ cup hoisin sauce

3 tablespoons chunky peanut butter

1 tablespoon fish sauce

1 teaspoon chili garlic sauce

⅓ cup chopped roasted peanuts

Heat a small saucepan over medium-high heat until hot. Add the oil, swirling to coat the bottom. Add the garlic and cook, stirring, until fragrant, about 10 seconds. Add the broth, hoisin sauce, peanut butter, fish sauce, and chili garlic sauce and bring to a boil. Reduce the heat to low, simmer for 3 minutes, and then remove from the heat. Set aside 1 tablespoon of the peanuts for garnish and stir the remainder into the sauce. Serve the sauce hot, warm, or at room temperature, garnished with the reserved nuts. Store in a covered container in the refrigerator; it will keep for up to 2 weeks.

MAKES ABOUT 1 ½ CUPS

HOMEMADE PONZU SAUCE

Not all supermarkets carry prebottled *ponzu* sauce, so I have put together a recipe that you can easily make at home. I've been known to add this tasty sauce to salad dressings and noodle dishes, or even to use it as a dip for tempura. This sauce is called for in a number of recipes in this book.

MAKES ABOUT 1½ CUPS

Zest of 1 lemon

½ cup mirin

½ cup fresh lemon juice

6 tablespoons soy sauce

½ cup sugar

1 tablespoon minced green onion

In a bowl, combine all the ingredients and stir until the sugar dissolves. Store in a covered container in the refrigerator; it will keep for up to 1 month.

ASIAN VINAIGRETTE

Use this delicious vinaigrette on your favorite salad greens. This recipe is a great example of how you can use ingredients from your Asian pantry any night of the week.

MAKES ABOUT ⅔ CUP

½ cup vegetable oil

¼ cup rice vinegar

1 tablespoon honey

2 teaspoons sesame oil

1 teaspoon grated ginger

1 clove garlic, minced

½ teaspoon prepared Chinese mustard

½ teaspoon salt

In a small bowl, combine all the ingredients and whisk until the honey dissolves. Store in a covered container in the refrigerator; it will keep for up to 3 weeks. Bring to room temperature and stir before using.

EASY AND TANGY SICHUAN PICKLED CUCUMBERS

For thin, uniform slices, use a food processor or a mandoline. The longer the cucumber slices marinate, the more intense the flavor. These tangy, spicy, and sweet cucumbers are a nice addition to sandwiches, salads, or for eating plain as a snack.

1 English cucumber, thinly sliced
1 tablespoon salt
1 cup rice vinegar
¼ cup soy sauce
¼ cup sugar
1 tablespoon red chili flakes

In a bowl, combine the cucumber and salt, toss to mix, and let stand for 10 minutes. Rinse, drain, pat dry, and place in a heat-proof bowl.

In a small saucepan, bring all the remaining ingredients to a boil. Remove from the heat and stir until the sugar dissolves. Pour over the cucumbers, stir, and cover with plastic wrap. Set aside for 10 minutes. Store in a covered container in the refrigerator; the cucumbers will keep for up to 1 month.

MAKES ABOUT 3 CUPS

SWEET-AND-SOUR SHREDDED CARROTS

This easy recipe is made even easier if you use the packaged preshredded carrots found in most supermarket produce aisles. I'll add these flavorful carrots to salads, sandwiches, or fresh spring rolls. For a twist, add 2 cups shredded daikon.

¾ cup rice vinegar
½ cup water
½ cup sugar
¼ teaspoon salt
3 cups shredded carrot
1 tablespoon fish sauce

In a small saucepan, combine the vinegar, water, sugar, and salt and bring to a boil. Remove from the heat and stir until the sugar dissolves.

Place the carrot in a heatproof bowl and pour the hot vinegar mixture over them. Add the fish sauce, stir to combine, and let cool. Store in a covered container in the refrigerator; the carrots will keep for up to 1 month.

MAKES ABOUT 3 CUPS

PLUM SAUCE FRUIT SALSA

I have been surprised at the number of chefs in Asia who use fresh fruit in their kitchens. This balanced combination of sweet fruit and savory ingredients creates a refreshing accompaniment to grilled fish and a bowl of steamed rice.

MAKES ABOUT 2 CUPS

2 **tablespoons plum sauce**

2 **tablespoons soy sauce**

2 **tablespoons fresh lemon juice**

1 **tablespoon honey**

1 **teaspoon chili garlic sauce**

1 **tablespoon chopped fresh mint**

1 **teaspoon grated ginger**

1 **red bell pepper,** seeded and chopped

1 **jalapeño chili,** minced

1 **ruby red grapefruit,** segmented (see page 16) and cut into chunks

1 **mango,** peeled, pitted, and cut into chunks

In a bowl, combine all the ingredients except the grapefruit and mango, and whisk until the honey dissolves. Add the fruits and mix lightly. Cover and refrigerate until ready to serve, up to 3 hours.

FRIED SHALLOTS

These shallots, commonly used in Southeast Asian cuisine, are a crisp, flavorful garnish for soups, salads, and my favorite use, *jook* (see page 80). Asian markets carry already-fried shallots, which will save you even more time. But if you decide to make them at home, it is important to take the time to slice them almost paper-thin and to separate the rings. Only then are you sure to get a crispy result when they hit the hot oil. This technique works well with garlic, too. If you don't have the time or the access to an Asian market, the fried onions available in every supermarket—the popular topping for the ever-present green bean casserole—are an acceptable substitute. To intensify their flavor, pop them into the oven for a few minutes to crisp up.

1 cup vegetable oil

8 walnut-sized shallots, thinly sliced in rings

MAKES ABOUT 1 CUP

In a small saucepan, heat the oil over medium-high heat to 375°F on a deep-frying thermometer. Working in small batches, add the shallots and cook, stirring, until golden brown, 3 to 4 minutes. Remove with a slotted spoon, drain on paper towels, and let cool. Store in an airtight container in a cool place for up to 1 month.

ZIPPY GINGER SYRUP

This spicy syrup can be added to fresh fruit for a quick dessert, or mixed with rum for a cocktail. The cayenne pepper intensifies the ginger flavor and gives the syrup dimension.

1 cup coarsely chopped ginger

2 cups water

2 cups sugar

¼ teaspoon cayenne pepper

MAKES ABOUT 2 CUPS

In a blender, combine the ginger and 1 cup of the water. Whirl until smooth, then pour into a heavy 2-quart pan. Add all the remaining ingredients and cook over low heat, stirring occasionally, until the sugar dissolves, about 10 minutes. Remove from the heat, let cool, and pour through a strainer into an airtight container. Store in the refrigerator for up to 2 months.

SMALL BITES & FIRST COURSES

YAN'S COCKTAIL NUTS

Serve this salty, sweet snack at your next cocktail party with refreshing Ho Chi Mojitos (page 226).

MAKES 5 CUPS

Seasoning Salt

- 2 teaspoons salt
- 1 tablespoon sugar
- ¼ teaspoon Chinese five-spice powder
- ¼ teaspoon cayenne pepper
- ⅛ teaspoon white pepper

- 5 cups unsalted mixed nuts such as walnuts, Spanish peanuts, natural almonds, and raw cashews
- ⅓ cup vegetable oil

Preheat the oven to 375°F.

To make the seasoning salt, in a small bowl, combine all the ingredients and mix well.

Place the nuts in an aluminum foil–lined baking pan. Drizzle with the oil and stir to coat evenly. Sprinkle the seasoning salt over the nuts and stir to coat evenly.

Toast, stirring once or twice, until the nuts are fragrant and lightly browned, 12 to 15 minutes.

Remove from the oven, let cool, and then store in an airtight container in the refrigerator for up to 1 month.

EDAMAME APPETIZER

Nothing could be easier and better for you than edamame (soybeans). You will find both fresh and frozen edamame in most supermarkets. If you use frozen ones, cook them for a few minutes longer. Remember, serve this with an empty bowl, for discarded pods, since you only eat the beans inside them. I love this fun finger food! Seasoned pepper is a blend of black pepper, onion, and red and green bell peppers. It is found in the spice aisle of most supermarkets.

MAKES 3 TO 4 SERVINGS

- 2 whole star anise
- ½ pound edamame in the pod
- 1 teaspoon salt
- ½ teaspoon seasoned pepper
- ¼ teaspoon Chinese five-spice powder

Bring a saucepan filled with water to a boil. Add the star anise and edamame, cover, remove from the heat, and set aside for 3 minutes. Drain, place in a bowl, and sprinkle with the salt, pepper, and five-spice powder. Toss until pods are evenly coated. Serve at once.

MARBLED TEA EGGS

When I was little, my grandmother would make this traditional dish, and I was always fascinated with the eggs' marbled appearance. They look cool and taste great! Make a double batch and keep the eggs in the refrigerator for snacking; store them in an airtight container for up to 1 week. Dark soy sauce will give you a richer color and flavor, but using regular soy sauce will result in eggs equally delicious. Serve these tasty treats in numerous ways: add them to a bowl of noodles, use them to garnish a salad, or eat them as a snack on a picnic.

8 eggs
1 green onion, coarsely chopped
2 teaspoons minced ginger
¼ cup regular soy sauce
¼ cup dark soy sauce
4 bags black tea
2 tablespoons packed dark brown sugar
½ teaspoon Chinese five-spice powder
3 whole star anise
1 cinnamon stick

MAKES 8 SERVINGS

In a large saucepan, place the eggs with water to cover and bring to a simmer over medium heat. Simmer, uncovered, for 10 minutes. Drain, then rinse the eggs with cold water until cool enough to handle. Gently tap each egg all over with a spoon until hairline cracks cover the entire shell.

Return the eggs to the pan. Add all the remaining ingredients and some water, if needed, to cover the eggs completely. Place over low heat, cover, and simmer for at least 15 minutes, or for up to 1 hour for more intense color. Remove from the heat, let the eggs cool in the liquid, and then refrigerate, still in the liquid, at least overnight or for up to 1 week.

To serve, remove the eggs from the liquid, peel them, and place in a serving bowl.

RICE PAPER WRAPS

Of all the recipes in this book, this is the most challenging. But practice makes perfect. The more comfortable you become handling rice paper, the easier it will be to shape these delicious low-fat rolls. Prep all the ingredients in advance, but roll just before serving. If you refrigerate the softened rice paper, it will toughen.

MAKES 8 WRAPS

4   ounces dried rice stick noodles

½   cup Sweet-and-Sour Shredded Carrots (page 37)

8   rice paper rounds, each about 8 inches in diameter

16   medium-sized cooked, peeled shrimp, cut in half lengthwise

4   leaves red-leaf lettuce, ribs removed and each leaf cut in half lengthwise

1   cup bean sprouts

16   fresh mint leaves

8   fresh cilantro sprigs

Peanut Dipping Sauce (page 35) or
Southeast Asian All-Purpose Dipping Sauce (page 35)

Bring a large pot filled with water to a boil over high heat. Add the noodles and cook until tender, about 3 minutes. Drain, rinse with cold water, and drain again. Cut into rough 3-inch lengths. Place in a bowl, add the carrots, and toss to combine.

To make each roll, place a rice paper round on a work surface and brush with warm water. Let stand until it becomes soft and pliable, about 30 seconds. Place 4 shrimp halves in a line across the round, positioning them 2 inches above the bottom edge. Top with a piece of lettuce, about ½ cup of the noodle mixture, 8 to 10 bean sprouts, 2 mint leaves, and 1 cilantro sprig. Distribute the ingredients in an even line, leaving a 1-inch border on each side. Fold the bottom edge of the wrapper over the filling and press down to make the filling compact. Fold in the sides, and then continue rolling to enclose completely. The roll should be tight.

Before serving, cut each roll in half. Serve with the dipping sauce.

HARVEST VEGETABLES WITH CURRY DIP

You can make this dip up to a day ahead, which allows more time for the flavors to blend. I prefer using Madras curry powder because it has a more complex flavor than other blends. Do not limit yourself to the listed vegetables. Select what your family enjoys the most and is easiest to prepare. I've noticed that most supermarkets have precut celery, carrots, and even jicama.

MAKES 8 SERVINGS

Curry Dip

1	cup mayonnaise
1	cup sour cream
2	tablespoons sweet chili sauce
1½	tablespoons soy sauce
1	tablespoon curry powder
½	teaspoon cayenne pepper
⅛	teaspoon Chinese five-spice powder

½	pound asparagus, tough ends trimmed
2	teaspoons salt
1	English cucumber
1	red bell pepper
½	pound sugar snap peas
½	pound baby carrots, trimmed

To make the dip, combine all the ingredients in a small bowl and mix well. Cover and chill before serving.

Bring a large saucepan filled with water to a boil. Add the asparagus and salt and cook until tender-crisp, about 2 minutes. Drain, rinse with cold water, and drain again. Pat dry with paper towels. Cut the cucumber into sticks about 3 inches long and ½ inch thick. Cut the bell pepper into strips. Chill the vegetables before serving.

Arrange the asparagus, cucumber, bell pepper, peas, and carrots on a serving platter. Serve with the chilled dip.

CRAB PUFFS

What's in a name? In many parts of North America, these puffs are instead called seafood wontons or crab Rangoon. Whichever name you use, follow the recipe, and you and your guests will be in for a special treat.

Filling

One 8-ounce package cream cheese, softened

2 green onions, minced

1 tablespoon finely chopped fresh mint

2 teaspoons minced ginger

1 tablespoon oyster-flavored sauce

1 teaspoon sesame oil

⅛ teaspoon white pepper

½ pound cooked or imitation crabmeat

40 wonton wrappers

Vegetable oil for deep-frying

Purchased sweet-and-sour sauce

MAKES 40 PUFFS

To make the filling, combine the cream cheese, green onions, mint, ginger, oyster-flavored sauce, sesame oil, and pepper in a bowl and mix well. Stir in the crabmeat.

To make each puff, place a rounded teaspoon of the filling in the center of a wonton wrapper. Brush the edges of the wrapper with water, fold the wrapper over the filling to form a triangle, and press the edges to seal.

Pour oil to a depth of 2 inches into a 2-quart saucepan and heat to 350°F on a deep-frying thermometer. Working in batches, add the puffs and deep-fry, turning occasionally, until golden brown, about 1 minute. Remove with a slotted spoon and drain on paper towels. Serve warm with sweet-and-sour sauce for dipping.

COOL SHRIMP WITH CHILI DIPPING SAUCE

Here, Asian seasonings give the Western shrimp cocktail a new twist. You can make your own *ponzu* sauce, or look for it in the Asian section of your grocery store. Be sure to have plenty of ice on hand to cool the shrimp in the cooking liquid.

MAKES 4 SERVINGS

2 cups water

1 cup dry white wine

4 quarter-sized slices ginger, lightly crushed

2 teaspoons fish sauce

2 teaspoons Ponzu Sauce (page 36)

1 pound large raw shrimp, peeled with tails intact and deveined

4 to 5 cups ice cubes

Dipping Sauce

1/2 cup mayonnaise

1 1/2 tablespoons soy sauce

1 tablespoon sweet chili sauce

1 1/2 teaspoons chili garlic sauce

1 teaspoon rice vinegar

Sliced pickled ginger for garnish

In a large saucepan, combine the water, wine, ginger, fish sauce, and Ponzu Sauce and bring to a boil over high heat. Add the shrimp and cook until they begin to curl and turn pink, 1 1/2 to 2 minutes. Remove from the heat and immediately add the ice to the pan to cool the liquid. When the liquid is cool, drain the shrimp and pat dry with paper towels.

Arrange on a serving plate.

To make the dipping sauce, combine all the ingredients in a small bowl and mix well.

Garnish the shrimp with the pickled ginger and serve with the dipping sauce.

POTSTICKERS WITH SPICY SOY DIPPING SAUCE

Yes, these take some time to prepare, but gather the family around to help. You can pleat the edges for a traditional look, or you can just fold the wrapper in half, which is much easier. I always double or triple the batch, and freeze what is not eaten that day for a quick appetizer or dinner in the future. Freeze the uncooked pot stickers in a single layer, then put them in a zippered heavy plastic bag. They will keep for a few months.

Filling

½	pound ground pork or ground turkey
2	green onions, minced
2	tablespoons minced bamboo shoots
1	teaspoon minced ginger
1	tablespoon cornstarch
2	teaspoons soy sauce
⅛	teaspoon white pepper

22	round potsticker wrappers
2	tablespoons vegetable oil
⅔	cup water
⅓	cup Spicy Soy Dipping Sauce (page 34)

MAKES 22 POTSTICKERS

To make the filling, combine all the ingredients in a large bowl and mix well.

To make each potsticker, place about a tablespoon of the filling in the center of a potsticker wrapper. Brush the edges of the wrapper with water, fold in half, and press the edges to seal. Set the potsticker on the work surface, seam side up, and press lightly to form a flat bottom.

Heat a nonstick frying pan over medium-high heat until hot. Add 1 tablespoon of the oil, swirling to coat the bottom. Add half of the potstickers, seam side up, and cook until the bottoms are golden brown, about 3 minutes. Add ⅓ cup of the water, cover, reduce the heat to low, and cook until the water is absorbed, about 3 minutes. Remove from the pan. Cook the remaining potstickers in the same way, first adding the remaining 1 tablespoon oil to the pan. Place the potstickers, browned side up, on a serving plate. Serve with the dipping sauce.

CHICKEN LETTUCE CUPS

I'm always coming up with different combinations of ingredients to make the ultimate recipe. Maybe I've found it this time—a new American favorite. If you have good knife skills, mince your own meat; the texture will be better. This filling can also be wrapped in a flour tortilla for an Asian-style burrito.

2   dried black mushrooms

½   pound ground chicken or ground turkey

1½   teaspoons cornstarch

2   teaspoons Chinese rice wine or dry sherry

Sauce

¼   cup hoisin sauce

2   teaspoons soy sauce

1½   teaspoons chili garlic sauce

1   teaspoon sesame oil

1   tablespoon vegetable oil

1   teaspoon minced ginger

1   clove garlic, minced

½   red bell pepper, seeded and finely chopped

½   cup finely chopped water chestnuts

2   teaspoons chopped fresh cilantro

8   small iceberg lettuce cups

In a small bowl, soak the mushrooms in warm water to cover until softened, about 15 minutes; drain. Discard the stems and coarsely chop the caps. Set aside.

In a bowl, combine the chicken, cornstarch, and wine and mix well. Let stand for 10 minutes.

To make the sauce, combine all the ingredients in a small bowl and mix well. Set aside.

Place a stir-fry pan over high heat until hot. Add the oil, swirling to coat the sides. Add the ginger and garlic and cook until fragrant, about 15 seconds. Add the chicken mixture and stir-fry until crumbly and no longer pink, about 2 minutes. Add the bell pepper, water chestnuts, and mushrooms and stir-fry until the bell pepper is soft, 1 to 2 minutes. Stir in the cilantro. Transfer to a serving plate.

To serve, arrange the lettuce cups on a plate and set alongside the sauce and the chicken mixture. To eat, each diner spreads a little sauce in a lettuce cup, spoons in some of the chicken mixture, folds the lettuce around the filling, and eats the packet out of hand.

SESAME CHICKEN STRIPS
WITH LEMON DIPPING SAUCE

My kids love these little chicken fingers and so will yours. They also take very little time to prepare. Or, you can purchase frozen already-cooked chicken strips and make only the sauce for an even quicker meal!

MAKES 4 SERVINGS

Marinade

- 1 tablespoon cornstarch
- 2 teaspoons fresh lemon juice
- 1 teaspoon soy sauce

- 1 pound chicken tenders or boneless, skinless breasts

Dipping Sauce

- ½ cup water
- ⅓ cup fresh lemon juice
- 2½ teaspoons packed brown sugar
- ½ teaspoon soy sauce
- Grated zest of 1 lemon
- 1½ tablespoons cornstarch dissolved in 2 tablespoons water

- Vegetable oil for deep-frying
- 1 cup panko
- 2 tablespoons sesame seeds
- 1 egg

To make the marinade, combine all the ingredients in a bowl and mix well. If using chicken tenders, leave whole. If using chicken breasts, cut crosswise into 1-inch-wide strips. Add the chicken to the marinade and stir to coat evenly. Let stand for 10 minutes.

To make the dipping sauce, combine all the ingredients except the cornstarch solution in a small saucepan. Set aside.

Pour oil to a depth of 2 inches into a 2-quart saucepan and heat to 350°F on a deep-frying thermometer. Mix the panko and sesame seeds in a shallow bowl. Lightly beat the egg in a second shallow bowl. One at a time, dip the chicken strips into the egg, drain briefly, and then coat with the panko mixture. As the chicken strips are coated, add them to the hot oil, a few at a time, and deep-fry, turning once, until golden brown, 2 to 3 minutes on each side. Remove with a slotted spoon and drain on paper towels.

Meanwhile, place the sauce over medium-high heat and bring to a boil. Cook, stirring, until the sugar dissolves, about 2 minutes. Add the cornstarch solution and cook, stirring, until the sauce boils and thickens, about 15 seconds. Pour the sauce into a bowl. Serve the chicken hot with the dipping sauce.

SOUTHEAST ASIAN MEATBALLS

Because texture is important in this recipe, I suggest you use an electric stand mixer with a paddle attachment to combine the meatball mixture. If you don't have one, use those biceps and simply beat the mixture with a wooden spoon until stiff. You must have a very smooth mixture to result in a dense meatball. These also make a great sandwich: serve on a crusty French roll with sliced onions and sprigs of cilantro.

Meatballs

- ½ pound ground pork
- ¼ pound medium-sized raw shrimp, peeled, deveined, and minced
- 1 tablespoon chopped green onion
- 1 teaspoon minced garlic
- 1 egg white
- 2 tablespoons soy sauce or fish sauce
- 2 tablespoons water
- 1 tablespoon cornstarch
- ¼ teaspoon black pepper

Sauce

- One 14½-ounce can diced tomatoes, undrained
- 1 tablespoon oyster-flavored sauce
- 2 teaspoons sugar
- 1½ teaspoons cornstarch dissolved in 1 tablespoon water

- 1 tablespoon chopped cilantro

To make the meatballs, combine all the ingredients in the bowl of an electric mixer. Using the paddle attachment, mix on medium speed until the mixture is homogeneous and stiff.

With wet hands, roll the meat mixture into walnut-sized balls, using about 2 tablespoons for each ball. Arrange the meatballs, without crowding, on a lightly greased heatproof plate.

Prepare a stir-fry pan for steaming (see page 16). Place the meatballs in the stir-fry pan, cover, and steam over high heat until the pork is cooked through, about 10 minutes. Test for doneness by cutting into a meatball. Meanwhile, make the sauce: In a small saucepan, combine all the ingredients and bring to a boil over medium-high heat. Cook, stirring occasionally, until the sauce thickens, about 1 minute.

Drizzle the hot sauce over the meatballs, garnish with cilantro, and serve.

NORTH VIETNAMESE–STYLE SPRING ROLLS

The flavors in these rolls will give you a taste of northern Vietnam, where cooks use black pepper, shallots, and fish sauce. Traditionally, the rolls are made with rice paper, but I've used the more readily available and easier to handle spring roll wrapper. This is not an egg roll wrapper. A spring roll wrapper is lighter and thinner.

MAKES 24 ROLLS

Filling

One 1½-ounce bundle dried bean thread noodles

2 dried wood ears

¾ pound ground pork or ground chicken

¼ cup chicken broth

2 walnut-sized shallots, minced

2 cloves garlic, minced

2 tablespoons chopped fresh cilantro

1 tablespoon sugar

1 tablespoon fish sauce

½ teaspoon black pepper

12 spring roll wrappers, cut in half on the diagonal

2 tablespoons flour mixed with ¼ cup water

vegetable oil for deep-frying

1 head red-leaf lettuce, leaves separated

⅓ cup Southeast Asian All-Purpose Dipping Sauce (page 35)

In separate bowls, soak the bean thread noodles and wood ears in warm water to cover until softened, about 10 minutes; drain. Cut the noodles into 2-inch lengths; cut the wood ears into narrow strips. In a large bowl, combine the filling ingredients and mix well.

To make each roll, place a triangular wrapper on a work surface with the long edge facing you. Spread ¼ cup of the filling in a band across the wrapper, positioning it 2 inches above the bottom and leaving a 2-inch border at either side. Fold the bottom edge of the wrapper over the filling, then fold in the right and left corners. Roll over once to enclose the filling. Brush the sides and tip of the triangle with the flour-water paste. Fold over to seal. Cover with a damp kitchen towel to prevent them from drying out.

Heat vegetable oil to 350°F on a deep-frying thermometer. Working in batches, add the rolls and deep-fry, turning the rolls, until they are golden brown and the filling is cooked, 4 to 5 minutes. Remove with a slotted spoon and drain on paper towels.

Serve the rolls warm with the lettuce and the dipping sauce. To eat, place a roll on a lettuce leaf, wrap the lettuce around the roll, dip it in the sauce, and eat out of hand.

PEPPERY CHICKEN WINGS

Have on hand a bunch of napkins for these messy wings and a few Asian beers to tame the spice. Double or even triple the recipe for the big football game.

MAKES 6 SERVINGS

12	chicken wings (about 2 pounds total)
3	tablespoons honey
1½	tablespoons soy sauce
1	green onion, minced
1	jalapeño chili, minced
1	teaspoon black pepper
½	teaspoon garlic powder
¼	teaspoon salt
¼	teaspoon Chinese five-spice powder
¼	teaspoon white pepper

Preheat the oven to 400°F.

Cut each chicken wing at joints. Discard the wing tips or reserve for making broth. Bring a large saucepan filled with water to a boil. Add the wings and cook for 3 minutes. Drain and pat dry with paper towels.

In a bowl, combine all the remaining ingredients, whisking to dissolve the honey. Add the wings and stir to coat evenly.

Arrange the wings in a single layer on an aluminum foil–lined baking pan. Bake for 10 minutes. Turn the wings over and continue to bake until the wings are tender, 10 to 15 minutes longer. Serve hot.

HONEY-GLAZED SPARERIBS

Don't confuse these ribs (pictured here with Rice Paper Wraps, page 44) with the 1-inch spareribs served in most Chinese restaurants. These are about 4 inches long. The ribs must be cut apart for quick cooking, and if you use the smaller ones, there are so many that they are too pesky to turn. Serve with Simple Sesame Noodles (page 204) and Flash-Fried Asparagus and Long Beans (page 175) for a delicious meal.

MAKES 4 TO 6 SERVINGS

1 side pork spareribs (about 2 pounds)

Marinade

¼ cup hoisin sauce

3 tablespoons soy sauce

3 tablespoons Chinese rice wine or dry sherry

1 tablespoon minced ginger

1 tablespoon minced garlic

1 teaspoon Chinese five-spice powder

Honey Glaze

3 tablespoons hoisin sauce

2 tablespoons honey

2 teaspoons sesame oil

Cut the side of ribs between the bones into individual pieces. Bring a large pot filled with water to a boil over high heat. Add the ribs and cook for 5 minutes, then pour into a colander to drain.

To make the marinade, combine all the ingredients in a large bowl and mix well. Add the ribs and stir to coat evenly. Let stand for 10 minutes; for a deeper flavor, cover and refrigerate overnight.

Preheat the oven to 400°F.

To make the glaze, combine all the ingredients in a small bowl and stir until the honey is dissolved. Set aside.

Lift the ribs from the marinade and place on a rack in an aluminum foil–lined baking pan; reserve the marinade.

Bake the ribs for 10 minutes. Turn the ribs over, baste with the reserved marinade, and bake for 5 minutes longer. Brush with the glaze and continue baking until the ribs are tender, about 5 minutes longer. Serve hot.

TANGY BEAN SPROUT SALAD

This is a nice side dish to serve with the Vietnamese Egg Custard (page 93) or Grilled Satay Chicken Tenders (page 141). Although a bit time-consuming, removing the root tips from the bean sprouts makes a more elegant presentation. In Asia, this step is eliminated: wander through the produce markets and you'll find barrels of bean sprouts with both ends already removed.

MAKES 4 SERVINGS

1 teaspoon sesame seeds

1 pound bean sprouts

½ English cucumber, julienned

1 teaspoon salt

3 tablespoons fresh lemon juice

1½ tablespoons honey

2 teaspoons fish sauce

1 teaspoon sesame oil

½ teaspoon chili garlic sauce

¾ cup shredded bamboo shoots

2 tablespoons shredded pickled ginger

½ cup Sweet-and-Sour Shredded Carrots (page 37)

In a small frying pan, toast the sesame seeds over medium heat, shaking the pan frequently, until lightly colored, 3 to 4 minutes. Immediately pour onto a plate to cool. In a bowl, combine the bean sprouts, cucumber, and salt. Let stand for 15 minutes. Place in a colander, rinse well with water, and drain. Turn out onto paper towels and pat dry. In a large bowl, combine the lemon juice, honey, fish sauce, sesame oil, sesame seeds, and chili garlic sauce. Stir until the honey is dissolved. Add the bean sprouts, cucumber, bamboo shoots, and pickled ginger and toss to coat evenly. Garnish with the carrots and serve.

CITRUS RICE NOODLES

Pair this light, refreshing salad with the bold, rich flavors of Glazed Grilled Pork Chops (page 168) or Lemon-Pepper Beef (page 152). If you want to make this ahead, keep the citrus separate from the noodles and refrigerate. Before assembly, dip the chilled noodles in a pot of boiling water for about 30 seconds, and then run under cold water to chill. Toss together all the ingredients for a quick assembly.

8   ounces dried rice stick noodles

Dressing

1   tablespoon fish sauce

1   tablespoon sesame oil

1   tablespoon chili garlic sauce

2   teaspoons honey

½   teaspoon salt

2   oranges, segmented (see page 16)

1   grapefruit, segmented (see page 16)

1   tablespoon chopped fresh mint

1   tablespoon chopped roasted peanuts

Bring a large pot filled with water to a boil over high heat. Add the noodles and cook until tender, about 3 minutes. Drain, rinse with cold water, and drain again. Cut into 4-inch lengths. Place in a large bowl.

To make the dressing, combine all the ingredients in a small bowl and mix well.

Pour the dressing over the noodles. Add the citrus and stir to coat evenly. Garnish with the mint and peanuts and serve.

MAKES 4 SERVINGS

POMELO, RADISH, AND SPINACH SALAD

The pomelo symbolizes abundance in Chinese New Year celebrations because the Chinese word for pomelo sounds like the word for "to have." Eating and sharing this ancestor to the grapefruit is like guaranteeing that you and your family will have an abundant life in the New Year. Substitute ruby red grapefruit when pomelo is not in season.

MAKES 4 SERVINGS

Dressing

- ¼ cup vegetable oil
- ¼ cup fresh lemon juice
- 2 tablespoons fresh orange juice
- 1 tablespoon sesame oil
- 1 tablespoon honey
- ¾ teaspoon chili garlic sauce

- ¼ cup pine nuts
- 1 pomelo, segmented (see page 16)
- 2½ cups packed baby spinach
- 3 red radishes, trimmed and thinly sliced
- One 8-ounce can sliced water chestnuts, drained
- ½ cup thinly sliced red onion
- 2 tablespoons thinly sliced crystallized ginger

To make the dressing, combine all the ingredients in a small bowl and whisk to blend. In a small frying pan, toast the pine nuts over medium heat, shaking the pan frequently, until lightly browned, 3 to 4 minutes. Pour onto a plate and let cool.

In a large bowl, combine the pomelo segments, spinach, radishes, water chestnuts, onion, crystallized ginger, and pine nuts. Pour the dressing over the salad, toss well, and serve.

ASPARAGUS ORANGE SALAD

In spring, when California's Central Valley asparagus harvest begins, I prepare this versatile vegetable Sichuan style. I cook it in boiling water, chill it in ice water, and then toss it in a tangy dressing. When asparagus is not in season, I use cooked long beans or green beans. You can prepare the salad components ahead of time, but wait until the last minute to add the dressing. Green vegetables lose their bright color if they stand in an acidic dressing too long.

MAKES 4 SERVINGS

1 pound asparagus
1 teaspoon vegetable oil
½ teaspoon salt

Dressing
¼ cup sweet chili sauce
2 tablespoons fresh lemon juice
2 teaspoons soy sauce
2 teaspoons sesame oil

1 orange, segmented **(see page 16)**
⅓ cup purchased glazed walnuts

Trim off the tough ends from the asparagus. Cut the spears into 1½-inch pieces. Pour water to a depth of 2 inches into a wide saucepan and bring to a boil over high heat. Add the oil, salt, and asparagus and cook until tender-crisp, 1 to 2 minutes. Drain, rinse with cold water, and drain again. Pat dry with paper towels and place in a bowl. Cover and chill until ready to serve.

To make the dressing, combine all the ingredients in a small bowl and mix well.

Just before serving, pour the dressing over the asparagus and stir lightly to coat evenly. Place on a serving plate and top with the orange segments. Sprinkle with the nuts and serve.

BACKYARD ASIAN COLESLAW

My backyard barbecue would not be complete without this coleslaw. Friends and family keep their eyes and mouths open for it. So, give this version a try at your next barbecue or picnic using your Asian pantry seasonings. If time is short, look for precut cabbage sold in most supermarkets.

Dressing

- ⅔ cup mayonnaise
- ¼ cup rice vinegar
- 2 tablespoons soy sauce
- 2 tablespoons sesame oil
- 2 tablespoons honey
- 1½ tablespoons wasabi paste
- 1 tablespoon chili garlic sauce

- 3 cups shredded napa cabbage
- 1½ cups bean sprouts
- ½ cup shredded carrot
- 8 ears baby corn, cut on the diagonal into 1-inch pieces
- 2 green onions, thinly sliced
- ⅓ pound small, cooked, peeled shrimp
- 2 tablespoons chopped toasted walnuts

To make the dressing, combine all the ingredients in a bowl and whisk to blend evenly. Cover and chill until serving.

In a large bowl, combine the cabbage, bean sprouts, carrot, baby corn, and green onions and toss to mix. Cover and chill until serving. To serve, pour the dressing over the salad and toss to coat evenly. Mound the shrimp in the center and sprinkle with the nuts. Serve at once.

MAKES 6 SERVINGS

WO TI'S GARLICKY ROMAINE SALAD

Rich, bold, and delicious, this salad complements Korean-Style Lamb Chops (page 162) or Grilled Satay Chicken Tenders (page 141) for a company dinner, or Great Wall Hoisin Pizza (page 126) for a casual family meal.

MAKES 4 SERVINGS

Dressing

- ½ cup pine nuts
- ¼ cup vegetable oil
- ¼ cup rice vinegar
- 1 tablespoon fish sauce
- 1 tablespoon sesame oil
- 3 cloves garlic, lightly crushed
- ¼ cup chopped fresh cilantro leaves and stems
- ¼ teaspoon white pepper

- ½ teaspoon salt
- ¼ teaspoon Chinese five-spice powder
- Vegetable oil for deep-frying
- 8 wonton wrappers, cut into ¼-inch-wide strips

- 1 avocado, peeled, pitted, and diced
- 5 cups torn romaine lettuce (about 10 ounces)
- 2 tablespoons Fried Shallots (page 38)
- 2 tablespoons fried garlic, prepared as for Fried Shallots (optional)

To make the dressing, in a small frying pan, toast the pine nuts over medium heat, shaking the pan frequently, until lightly browned, 3 to 4 minutes. Place the nuts in a blender with all the remaining ingredients. Whirl until thoroughly combined.

In a small bowl, mix together the salt and five-spice powder.

Pour oil to a depth of 2 inches into a 2-quart saucepan and heat to 350°F on a deep-frying thermometer. Working in batches, add the wonton strips and deep-fry until golden brown, about 30 seconds. Remove with a slotted spoon, drain briefly on paper towels, and then place in large bowl. Sprinkle the salt mixture over the strips and toss gently to coat evenly.

To assemble salad, place the avocado, lettuce, shallots, and garlic (if using) in a large bowl. Pour half of the dressing over the lettuce and toss to coat evenly. Garnish the salad with the wonton strips. Pass the remaining dressing at the table.

CRISP APPLE AND SHRIMP SALAD

I love the green papaya or mango salad that is served in many Thai and Vietnamese restaurants, but the green fruit is not always easy to find. So I tried the salad with my family's favorite fruit, tart green apple. What a delicious result!

Dressing

- ¼ cup fresh orange juice
- 2 tablespoons fresh lime juice
- 2 tablespoons oyster-flavored sauce
- 2 teaspoons sugar
- 1 teaspoon minced ginger
- ½ teaspoon chili garlic sauce

- 3 cups mixed salad greens
- 12 medium-sized cooked, peeled shrimp
- 1 large green apple, cored and cut into matchsticks (about 2 cups)
- ⅓ cup fresh cilantro leaves
- ¼ cup finely shredded fresh basil
- 2 tablespoons Fried Shallots (page 38)

To make the dressing, combine all the ingredients in a bowl and stir until the sugar dissolves.

Place the salad greens in a large bowl. Drizzle 2 tablespoons of the dressing over the greens and toss to coat evenly. Arrange the greens on a serving plate. Put the shrimp, apple, cilantro, and basil in the same bowl. Add the remaining dressing and toss to coat evenly. Spoon the shrimp mixture over the dressed greens. Garnish with the shallots and serve.

MAKES 4 SERVINGS

GRILLED BEEF AND CABBAGE SALAD

The aromatic fresh herbs in this salad create flavor with very little fat, while the earthy shiitake mushrooms add complexity.

Dressing

- ⅓ cup fresh lemon juice
- 3 tablespoons soy sauce
- 2 tablespoons vegetable oil
- 1½ tablespoons sweet chili sauce
- 1 lemongrass stalk, bottom 4 inches only, minced
- ½ cup thinly sliced shallots
- ⅓ cup chopped fresh cilantro
- ⅓ cup chopped fresh mint
- Grated zest of 1 lemon
- 1 tablespoon sugar

- ¾ pound flank steak
- 2 teaspoons soy sauce
- ½ teaspoon black pepper
- 1 teaspoon vegetable oil

- 4 cups shredded napa cabbage
- 1½ cups thinly sliced fresh shiitake mushrooms (about 3½ ounces)

To make the dressing, combine all the ingredients in a small bowl and mix well. Let stand for 5 minutes for the flavors to blend.

Season the beef with the soy sauce and pepper. Place a grill pan over medium-high heat until hot. Brush the pan with the oil. Place the beef on the pan and cook, turning once, until browned on both sides but still pink in the center, 3 to 4 minutes on each side. Remove from the pan, place on a cutting board, and cover with aluminum foil, shiny side down. Let stand for 10 minutes, then cut the meat across the grain on the diagonal into thin slices.

In a large bowl, combine the cabbage and mushrooms. Pour all but 2 tablespoons of the dressing over the cabbage mixture and toss well. Place on a serving plate. In the same bowl, toss the meat slices with the remaining 2 tablespoons dressing. Spoon the meat over the cabbage and serve.

EAST-WEST GAZPACHO

Don't worry if you are not as fast with a cleaver as I am. Knife skills are not critical for this refreshing soup, as everything is puréed in a blender. Also, here's another shortcut: I use canned tomatoes because their flavor is consistent year-round. But when tomatoes are sweet, juicy, and at their peak, you can use 1½ pounds fresh tomatoes, peeled and chopped, instead.

MAKES 4 TO 6 SERVINGS

One **28-ounce can tomatoes,** undrained

1½ **tablespoons thinly sliced ginger**

2 **cloves garlic**

1 **small red bell pepper,** seeded and coarsely chopped **(about 1 cup)**

1 **cucumber,** peeled, seeded, and coarsely chopped **(about 1¾ cups)**

½ **red onion,** coarsely chopped

3 **tablespoons chopped fresh cilantro leaves and stems**

2 **tablespoons rice vinegar**

2 **tablespoons fresh lemon juice**

1 **tablespoon oyster-flavored sauce**

1 **tablespoon chili garlic sauce**

1 **tablespoon sesame oil**

¾ **teaspoon salt**

Fresh cilantro sprigs for garnish

In a blender, combine ¼ cup of the tomato juice, the ginger, and the garlic. Whirl until smooth. Add the tomatoes and their remaining juice and all the remaining ingredients except the cilantro sprigs. Whirl until smooth. Pour into a bowl, cover, and chill well.

To serve, ladle the soup into chilled bowls and garnish with cilantro sprigs.

ASIAN CUCUMBER BISQUE

Adding cucumber at the end of the cooking process makes this soup explode with fresh flavor. For a traditional Chinese version, look for fuzzy melons, cylindrical green vegetables about 6 inches long, in Asian markets. Mild in flavor, they are covered with fine hairlike fuzz and must be peeled before cooking.

2 English cucumbers or fuzzy melons

2 teaspoons vegetable oil

½ yellow onion, minced

3 cups vegetable broth

1 cup unsweetened coconut milk

½ cup cooked long-grain rice

1 tablespoon oyster-flavored sauce

½ teaspoon salt

⅛ teaspoon white pepper

1 tablespoon chopped fresh cilantro

2 tablespoons Fried Shallots (page 38)

Peel the cucumbers or fuzzy melons. Dice enough cucumber to measure ½ cup and set aside for garnish. Coarsely chop the remainder. If using fuzzy melons, coarsely chop both melons.

Place a large saucepan over medium-high heat until hot. Add the oil, swirling to coat the bottom. Add the onion and cook, stirring, until fragrant, about 30 seconds. Add the broth, coconut milk, rice, oyster-flavored sauce, salt, pepper, and fuzzy melons (if using) and bring to a boil. Reduce the heat to low and simmer, uncovered, for 10 minutes. If using cucumbers, add the coarsely chopped cucumbers now and remove the pan from the heat. Working in batches, purée the soup in a blender until smooth. Return the soup to the pan and reheat to serving temperature.

Ladle the soup into bowls and garnish with the diced cucumber (if using), cilantro, and shallots.

MAKES 4 SERVINGS

COCONUT SQUASH SOUP

You can use any firm winter squash to make this soup, but I like butternut squash because of its sweet flavor and creamy texture. As a time-saver, look for fresh diced, peeled squash sold in 1-pound bags in the produce aisle. Use the whole bag even if it measures out to be slightly more than 2 cups.

MAKES 4 TO 6 SERVINGS

5 cups chicken broth

2 cups diced, peeled butternut squash

1 cup unsweetened coconut milk

½ yellow onion, diced

1 tablespoon grated ginger

8 snow peas, strings removed

2 tablespoons soy sauce

⅛ teaspoon white pepper

1 tablespoon chopped fresh cilantro

In a saucepan, combine the broth, squash, coconut milk, onion, and ginger over high heat. Bring to a boil, reduce the heat to low, and simmer, uncovered, until the squash is tender, about 10 minutes.

Add the snow peas, soy sauce, and pepper and cook until the snow peas are tender-crisp, about 1½ minutes.

Ladle the soup into bowls, sprinkle with the cilantro, and serve.

MISO SOUP

Protein-rich miso, or fermented soybean paste, gives this quick Japanese soup an appealing aroma and taste. Look for instant dashi granules, bouillon cubes, or liquid, or use chicken broth in place of the dashi and garnish with strips of nori.

6 cups dashi or chicken broth

1 tablespoon grated ginger

$1/2$ cup shredded carrot

$1/4$ cup sliced bamboo shoots

4 fresh shiitake mushrooms, stems discarded and caps thinly sliced

$1/3$ cup mirin

$1/3$ cup white miso

One-half 16-ounce package soft or firm tofu, drained and cut into $1/4$-inch cubes

1 cup cooked rice stick noodles, cut into 2-inch lengths

2 green onions, cut into $1/2$-inch lengths

In a saucepan, combine the dashi and ginger and bring to a boil over high heat. Add the carrot, bamboo shoots, mushrooms, and mirin, reduce the heat to low, cover, and simmer until the carrot is tender, about 5 minutes.

Stir in the miso, blending until smooth. Add the tofu, noodles, and green onions and simmer over low heat until the tofu is heated through, about 2 minutes.

Ladle the soup into bowls and serve.

CREAMY MUSHROOM SOUP

Asian cooks in North America have used dried shiitake mushrooms for years. Now these flavorful mushrooms are sold fresh in many supermarkets, and this creamy soup is a delicious way to showcase their woodsy flavor. Like their dried counterparts, the stems of fresh shiitakes are tough and should be discarded.

4   dried black mushrooms

8   large fresh shiitake mushrooms

5   large button mushrooms

1   tablespoon vegetable oil

1   tablespoon minced ginger

½   yellow onion, diced

4   cups chicken broth

3   tablespoons oyster-flavored sauce

⅛   teaspoon white pepper

1   cup whipping cream or half-and-half

2   tablespoons cornstarch dissolved in
2 tablespoons water

In a small bowl, soak the dried mushrooms in warm water to cover until softened, about 15 minutes; drain. Discard the stems and quarter the caps. Discard the shiitake mushroom stems and slice the caps; reserve a few slices for garnish. Slice the button mushroom caps and stems.

Place a large saucepan over high heat until hot. Add the oil, swirling to coat the bottom. Add the ginger and onion and cook, stirring, until the onion is translucent, about 1 minute. Add the mushrooms and cook, stirring, until tender, 3 to 4 minutes. Add the broth, oyster-flavored sauce, and pepper and bring to a boil. Reduce the heat to low and simmer, uncovered, for 5 minutes to blend the flavors. Working in batches, purée the soup in a blender until smooth. Return the soup to the pan and bring to a simmer over medium heat. Stir in the cream and cook until the soup is thoroughly heated but not boiling. Add the cornstarch solution and cook, stirring, until the soup bubbles and thickens slightly, about 1 minute.

Ladle the soup into bowls, garnish with the reserved mushrooms slices, and serve.

EGG FLOWER CORN SOUP

This is my day-after-Thanksgiving soup. I simmer the turkey bones to make a rich broth and shred the meat for the soup. Year-round, this soup is quick to make with chicken broth. For a special occasion, use cooked lobster meat or crabmeat or raw scallops in place of the poultry. Add the eggs at the very end and don't stir too much. You want them to remain in large pieces that almost look like flowers floating in the soup.

MAKES 4 TO 6 SERVINGS

5 cups turkey or chicken broth

1 cup shredded cooked turkey or chicken

One 14½-ounce can cream-style corn

1 cup raw corn kernels (cut from 1 large ear corn)

¼ cup coarsely chopped water chestnuts

1½ tablespoons oyster-flavored sauce

2 teaspoons sesame oil

¼ teaspoon white pepper

3 tablespoons cornstarch dissolved in ⅓ cup water

2 eggs, lightly beaten

1 green onion, thinly sliced

In a large saucepan, bring the broth to a boil over high heat. Add the turkey, cream-style corn, raw corn kernels, water chestnuts, oyster-flavored sauce, sesame oil, and pepper. Return to a boil and cook for 3 minutes. Add the cornstarch solution and cook, stirring, until the soup boils and thickens slightly, about 1½ minutes. Remove from the heat and slowly drizzle in the eggs while gently stirring constantly with a spoon to form egg flowers. Ladle the soup into bowls, garnish with the green onion, and serve.

PINEAPPLE HOT-AND-SOUR SOUP

You can make this aromatic soup without kaffir lime leaves, but if you do find them in an Asian or specialty market, buy more than you need, slip them into a zippered heavy plastic bag, and freeze. You may become so addicted to their lemony aroma, as I have, that you'll decide to plant a kaffir lime tree in your garden or greenhouse. For a Southeast Asian meal, serve with Fish and Long Bean Stir-fry (page 116) and Hue-Style Fried Rice (page 193).

MAKES 4 SERVINGS

Broth

- 6 **cups chicken broth**
- 1 **lemongrass stalk,** bottom 4 inches only, cut crosswise into thirds and crushed
- 2 **kaffir lime leaves,** thinly sliced **(optional)**
- 1 **small red or green jalapeño chili,** thinly sliced
- 1 **tablespoon sugar**

- ½ **pound medium-sized raw shrimp,** peeled and deveined
- 1 **small tomato,** cut into wedges
- 1 **cup bean sprouts**
- One **8-ounce can pineapple chunks,** in natural juice
- ½ **cup straw mushrooms**
- 2 **green onions,** thinly sliced on the diagonal
- 3 **tablespoons fish sauce or 2 tablespoons oyster-flavored sauce**
- ⅓ **cup fresh lime juice**

To make the broth, combine the chicken broth, lemongrass, lime leaves, chili, and sugar in a large saucepan over high heat and bring to a boil. Reduce the heat to low, cover, and simmer until the broth is lightly flavored, about 10 minutes. If desired, strain and discard the seasonings and return the broth to the pan.

Bring the broth to a boil over high heat. Add the shrimp, tomato, bean sprouts, pineapple and juice, and straw mushrooms and cook, stirring occasionally, until the shrimp turn pink, about 2 minutes.

Remove the pan from the heat and stir in the green onions, fish sauce, and lime juice.

Ladle into bowls and serve.

CRAB AND ASPARAGUS SOUP

Long ago, when the French introduced white asparagus to Vietnam, local cooks used traditional cooking techniques to weave this new ingredient into their cuisine. Here, it is used in a soup that combines fresh flavors and contrasting textures. If you can't find canned white asparagus, increase the amount of fresh asparagus to 1½ pounds and cook all of the spears as directed in the first step.

MAKES 4 TO 6 SERVINGS

10 fresh asparagus

1 tablespoon vegetable oil

2 green onions, chopped

1 teaspoon minced ginger

5 cups chicken broth

One 15-ounce can white asparagus, drained and cut on the diagonal into ½-inch pieces

½ pound cooked crabmeat, flaked

3 tablespoons soy sauce

⅛ teaspoon white pepper

1 tablespoon cornstarch dissolved in 2 tablespoons water

1 egg, lightly beaten

2 tablespoons chopped fresh cilantro

Trim off the tough ends from the fresh asparagus. Cut the spears into ½-inch pieces, leaving the tips in 1½-inch lengths. Bring a saucepan filled with water to a boil over high heat, add the asparagus, and cook until tender, 2 to 3 minutes. Drain, rinse with cold water, and drain again. Set aside the tips to use for garnish.

Place the same pan over medium-high heat until hot. Add the oil, swirling to coat the bottom. Add the green onions and ginger and cook, stirring, until fragrant, about 30 seconds. Add the broth, the cooked fresh asparagus, the white asparagus, crabmeat, soy sauce, and pepper and bring to a boil over high heat. Add the cornstarch solution and cook, stirring, until the soup boils and thickens slightly, about 1 minute. Remove from the heat and slowly drizzle in the egg while stirring constantly with a spoon to form egg flowers.

Ladle the soup into bowls, garnish with the reserved asparagus tips and the cilantro, and serve.

RIVER FISH DILL-TOMATO SOUP

Catfish fillets are my choice for this soup. Mild in flavor, the fillets are boneless, skinless, and take only a minute to slice. For a light lunch, add a bowl of steamed rice, or buy extra fish and serve with Fish Fried Rice (page 192) and Ginger Chicken (page 127) for a complete meal.

MAKES 4 TO 6 SERVINGS

6 **cups chicken broth**

1 **walnut-sized shallot,** cut into thin rings

2/3 **pound catfish fillets,** thinly sliced

2 **tomatoes,** each cut into 6 wedges

1 **tablespoon chopped fresh dill**

1 1/2 **tablespoons fish sauce**

3/4 **teaspoon sugar**

1/4 **teaspoon black pepper**

Fresh dill sprigs for garnish

In a saucepan, combine the broth and shallot and bring to a boil over high heat. Add the fish, reduce the heat to medium, and simmer for 1 minute. Skim the foam off the top of the broth. Add the tomatoes, chopped dill, fish sauce, sugar, and pepper. Cook until the fish turns opaque and the tomatoes soften, 2 to 3 minutes.

Ladle the soup into bowls, garnish with dill sprigs, and serve.

DUCK AND CABBAGE SOUP

If you live near a Chinese deli, pick up a roast duck or two and shred and freeze the meat for quick meals. You can substitute roast chicken for the duck, just add 1 whole star anise to the broth. I blanch canned bamboo shoots to eliminate their slightly tinny flavor, but you can omit this step if you purchase fresh water-packed bamboo shoots.

MAKES 4 TO 6 SERVINGS

4 **cups water**

2/3 **cup sliced bamboo shoots**

6 **cups chicken broth**

2 **cups thinly sliced napa cabbage**

1 **cup shredded roast duck meat**

One 3 1/2-**ounce package enoki mushrooms,** roots trimmed

In a saucepan, bring the water to a boil. Add the bamboo shoots and boil for 1 1/2 minutes; drain. In the same pan, bring the broth to a simmer over medium-high heat. Add the cabbage, duck meat, bamboo shoots, enoki and shiitake mushrooms, and soy sauce.

Simmer for 10 minutes to blend the flavors.

4 **fresh shiitake mushrooms,** stems discarded
  and caps thinly sliced

2 **tablespoons soy sauce**

2 **green onions,** thinly sliced on the diagonal

1 **teaspoon sesame oil**

Add the green onions and sesame oil and simmer for 1 minute.

Ladle the soup into bowls and serve.

TEA-FLAVORED CHICKEN-WALNUT SOUP

Have you had a soup that tastes good and is also good for you? In China, walnuts are believed to enhance energy and are used in soup as a tonic. The nuts are blanched in water first, so that their natural color will not darken the broth.

4 **dried black mushrooms**

1 **cup walnuts**

1½ **cups water**

3 **bags oolong tea**

4 **cups chicken broth**

1 **whole chicken leg,** cut apart at joint

2 **tablespoons chopped ginger**

2 **green onions,** cut into 2-inch lengths

1 **cup shredded jicama or daikon**

¼ **cup Chinese rice wine or dry sherry**

¾ **teaspoon salt**

⅛ **teaspoon white pepper**

1 **teaspoon sesame oil**

MAKES 4 TO 6 SERVINGS

In a small bowl, soak the mushrooms in warm water until softened, about 15 minutes; drain. Discard stems, quarter caps, and set aside. Bring a saucepan filled with water to a boil over high heat. Add the walnuts and boil for 3 minutes. Drain, rinse with cold water, and drain again. Set aside.

In the same pan, bring the 1½ cups water to a boil. Remove from the heat, drop in the tea bags, and let steep for 4 minutes. Discard the tea bags. Add the broth to the tea and bring to a simmer over low heat. Add the chicken and ginger and simmer for 10 minutes. Add the mushrooms, green onions, jicama, and wine and simmer until the chicken is tender, about 15 minutes longer.

Remove the chicken from the broth and let cool. Shred the meat and, if desired, thinly slice the skin. Return the chicken to the broth and add the walnuts, salt, pepper, and sesame oil and heat to serving temperature.

Ladle the soup into bowls and serve.

QUICK JOOK

Jook (the Cantonese name), or congee, is served throughout China for breakfast, lunch, and dinner, and even as a midnight snack. Every cook has his or her secret recipe for the soup. Some versions have distinct grains of rice; in others, the grains have broken down completely and the soup is smooth and creamy. This latter style comes from long, slow cooking. The key to giving this bland soup a punch of flavor is the garnish.

MAKES 6 TO 8 SERVINGS

2　cups cooked long-grain rice
5　cups chicken broth
5　cups water
2　teaspoons minced ginger
½　pound ground beef
1　teaspoon cornstarch

Garnishes
2　green onions, thinly sliced on the diagonal
　Fried Shallots (page 38)
　Soy sauce
　Sesame oil

In a large saucepan, combine the rice, broth, water, and ginger and bring to a boil over high heat. Reduce the heat to low and simmer, stirring occasionally, until the rice is soft and the broth is slightly creamy, 20 to 25 minutes. In a small bowl, combine the beef and cornstarch. Using a whisk, mix the beef into the soup and simmer until the beef is no longer pink, 5 to 6 minutes.

Ladle the soup into bowls. Garnish with the green onions and shallots and with a drizzle of soy sauce and sesame oil and serve.

BACK COUNTRY MUSHROOM-DAIKON SOUP

Here is a comfort food served by every Chinese mother, including mine. Typically the soup is flavored with dried shrimp, an ingredient sold in Asian markets, but you can use ½ cup bottled clam juice in place of the shrimp to give the soup a taste of the sea. Paired with a bowl of steamed rice, this makes a quick lunch.

8   dried black mushrooms

2   quarts (8 cups) chicken broth

¾   pound country-style pork ribs, cut between the bones

8   button mushrooms, quartered

3   green onions, cut into 2-inch lengths

4   quarter-sized ginger slices

¼   cup dried shrimp (optional)

½   pound daikon, peeled and cut into ¼-inch-thick rounds

1   teaspoon salt

½   teaspoon white pepper

In a small bowl, soak the mushrooms in warm water to cover until softened, about 15 minutes; drain. Discard the stems and cut the caps in half.

In a large pot, bring the broth to a boil over high heat. Add the ribs and cook for 3 minutes. Skim the foam off the top of the broth. Add the black and button mushrooms, green onions, ginger, dried shrimp, daikon, salt, and pepper and bring to a boil. Cover, reduce the heat to medium–low, and simmer until the daikon is tender and the ribs are cooked through, about 20 minutes.

Ladle the soup into bowls and serve.

BEEF RICE SOUP

The next time you cook rice, double the amount. When the rice is cold, pack it in 1- to 2-cup portions in zippered heavy plastic bags, flatten the bags, and freeze. Before making this soup, or any time you need a rice accompaniment, reheat a bag of frozen rice in the microwave oven for 1 to 2 minutes, then use as directed in the recipe.

Marinade

3   tablespoons soy sauce

1   tablespoon cornstarch

¼   teaspoon white pepper

½   pound lean ground beef

3   cups chicken broth

One 14-½-ounce can beef broth

1   yellow onion, finely chopped

1½   cups cooked long-grain rice

2   tablespoons Fried Shallots (page 38)

2   tablespoons chopped fresh cilantro

To make the marinade, combine all the ingredients in a bowl and mix well. Add the beef and again mix well.

In a saucepan, combine the chicken and beef broths and the onion and bring to a boil over high heat. Add the beef and stir to separate. Reduce the heat to medium and simmer for 5 minutes. Add the rice, stir to separate the grains, and simmer until heated through, 2 to 3 minutes.

Ladle the soup into bowls, top with the shallots and cilantro, and serve.

MAIN COURSES

LONG BEAN AND TOFU STIR-FRY

When I was young, my grandmother would often prepare a quick and easy dish like this. In my version, I sometimes deep-fry the tofu to give it a different texture. Serve with Grilled Miso-Glazed Eggplant (page 176) and Quick Glutinous Rice (page 33).

Sauce

½	cup vegetable broth
1½	tablespoons fish sauce
2	teaspoons chili garlic sauce
1	teaspoon sugar

1	tablespoon vegetable oil
½	yellow onion, chopped
¾	pound Chinese long beans, cut into 2-inch lengths
½	red bell pepper, seeded and cut into thin strips
One	14-ounce package firm tofu, drained and cut into ½-inch cubes

To make the sauce, combine all the ingredients in a small bowl and mix well.

Place a stir-fry pan over high heat until hot. Add the oil, swirling to coat the sides. Add the onion and cook, stirring, until slightly wilted, about 30 seconds. Add the long beans and stir-fry for 2½ minutes, adding a few drops of water if the pan appears dry. Add the bell pepper, tofu, and sauce and cook, stirring, until beans are tender, 2 to 3 minutes longer.

Transfer to a serving plate and serve.

SIMPLE STEAMED TOFU

No dish can be simpler. This takes only minutes to put together. When steaming, I prefer a bamboo steamer, but you can also cover a microwave-safe dish with plastic wrap and heat the tofu in the microwave. *Furikake* is a Japanese seasoning mixture that is a combination of toasted nori, sesame seeds, and spices. If you can't find it in your Asian grocery store, toast some nori and finely shred it, then combine it with toasted sesame seeds.

MAKES 4 SERVINGS

Sauce

- 1 tablespoon soy sauce
- 2 teaspoons sesame oil
- 1 teaspoon chili garlic sauce
- 1 teaspoon sugar

One 16-ounce package soft tofu
- 1 green onion, thinly sliced on the diagonal
- 2 teaspoons *furikake* or mixture of toasted nori strips and sesame seeds

To make the sauce, combine all the ingredients in a small bowl and mix well.

Drain the tofu and cut into ½-inch-thick slices. Place in a wide, shallow heatproof bowl. Prepare a stir-fry pan for steaming (see page 16). Place the bowl in the stir-fry pan, cover, and steam over high heat until heated through, 3 to 4 minutes.

Remove the bowl from the pan and spoon off the liquid from the bowl. Pour the sauce over the tofu. Sprinkle with the green onion and *furikake* and serve.

TOFU PORK PILLOWS

Here's my Asian version of the French *quenelle*. It is also an interesting way to eat healthful tofu. Be sure to mash the tofu and meat together well with your hands as you want the mixture to be homogeneous. You can make these up to 2 to 3 hours in advance and cover and refrigerate them until you are ready to cook.

One 14-ounce package firm tofu

Sauce

- ⅓ cup chicken broth
- ⅓ cup Chinese rice wine or dry sherry
- ¼ cup soy sauce
- ¼ cup rice vinegar
- 2 tablespoons sugar

- ½ pound ground pork
- 2 tablespoons cornstarch
- 1 tablespoon chopped fresh cilantro
- 2 teaspoons minced ginger
- 2 teaspoons sesame oil
- 2 tablespoons vegetable oil

Drape a piece of cheesecloth or a clean dish towel in a colander. Drain the tofu. With clean hands, crumble the tofu into the cheesecloth. Bring the ends of the cloth together and squeeze to remove excess liquid from the tofu. To make the sauce, combine all the ingredients in a small bowl and mix well. Set aside. In a large bowl, combine the tofu, pork, cornstarch, cilantro, ginger, and sesame oil. Stir rapidly with a wooden spoon until smooth. To shape each pillow, scoop up about 3 tablespoons of the tofu mixture with a soup spoon, then smooth the top with a table knife so it forms an oval. With the knife tip, push the oval onto a lightly oiled plate. Repeat with the remaining mixture, making 18 pillows. Place a wide frying pan, with lid, over high heat until hot. Add the vegetable oil, swirling to coat the bottom. Add the tofu pillows and cook, turning once, until golden brown, about 2 minutes. Add the sauce, reduce the heat to low, cover, and cook until the sauce has reduced slightly and the tofu pillows are cooked through, about 4 minutes.
Using a slotted utensil, transfer the pillows to a serving plate. Pour the sauce over the top and serve.

TOFU AND THREE MUSHROOM STIR-FRY

Firm tofu is easier to handle than soft tofu when stir-frying, but if you are gentle with the spoon, give the softer-textured variety a try.

Sauce

½ cup vegetable broth

3 tablespoons oyster-flavored sauce

1 teaspoon dark soy sauce or regular soy sauce

---

1 tablespoon vegetable oil

½ yellow onion, diced

2 cloves garlic, minced

One 14-ounce package firm tofu, drained and cut into ¾-inch cubes

5 button mushrooms, quartered

½ cup straw mushrooms

8 oyster mushrooms, ends trimmed but left whole

1 teaspoon cornstarch dissolved in 1 tablespoon water

To make the sauce, combine all the ingredients in a small bowl and mix well.

Heat a stir-fry pan over high heat until hot. Add the oil, swirling to coat the sides. Add the onion and garlic and cook, stirring, until the onion is translucent, about $1\frac{1}{2}$ minutes. Add the tofu, all the mushrooms, and the sauce, reduce heat to medium, cover, and cook until the mushrooms are tender, 2 to 3 minutes. Add the cornstarch solution and cook, stirring, until sauce boils and thickens slightly, about 20 seconds.

Transfer to a serving plate and serve.

MAKES 4 SERVINGS

VEGETABLE AND TOFU GREEN CURRY

An authentic curry recipe would not call for a cornstarch solution to thicken the sauce, but I prefer a thicker sauce that clings to the rice. This would typically be achieved with extra cooking time, but cornstarch speeds the process. If you prefer meat or seafood, replace the tofu with ½ pound pork, shrimp, or chicken. As with all curries, the flavor will have mellowed after a day. Serve the curry with steamed white rice (page 32).

MAKES 4 TO 6 SERVINGS

½ cup water

3 tablespoons green curry paste

One 13 ½-ounce can unsweetened coconut milk

1 tablespoon fish sauce

2 teaspoons fresh lime juice

2 tablespoons sugar

½ teaspoon salt

1 Asian eggplant, cut on the diagonal into ½-inch-thick slices

½ pound green beans, cut into 2-inch lengths

One 14-ounce package firm tofu, drained and cut into ¾-inch cubes

1 tomato, cut into bite-sized pieces

¼ cup sliced bamboo shoots

1 teaspoon cornstarch dissolved in 2 teaspoons water

In a 3-quart saucepan, bring the water to a boil over high heat. Whisk in the curry paste, reduce the heat to medium, and simmer for 1 minute. Add the coconut milk, fish sauce, lime juice, sugar, salt, eggplant, and green beans and mix well. Simmer until the beans are tender-crisp, 8 to 10 minutes.

Add the tofu, tomato, and bamboo shoots and cook until the tofu is heated through and eggplant is tender, 2 to 3 minutes. Add the cornstarch solution and cook, stirring, until the sauce boils and thickens, about 1 minute. Transfer to a serving bowl and serve.

CURRIED COCONUT POTPIE

It's surprising how many different cuisines use curry: Thai, Indian, Malaysian, Singaporean, and Chinese, to name only a few. Some are pastes made from fresh ingredients, while others are a mixture of ground spices. Serve this dish with a crisp green salad tossed in Asian Vinaigrette (page 36) and Five-Spice Pineapple Banana Split (page 218).

MAKES 4 SERVINGS

Coconut Curry Sauce

One 13½-ounce can unsweetened coconut milk

⅔ cup evaporated milk

¼ cup water

1½ tablespoons soy sauce

2 teaspoons curry powder

1 teaspoon sugar

1 teaspoon ground turmeric

¼ teaspoon white pepper

1 tablespoon cornstarch dissolved in 2 tablespoons water

1 tablespoon vegetable oil

1 clove garlic, minced

1 teaspoon minced ginger

½ pound boneless, skinless chicken breast or thigh or pressed tofu, cut into ½-inch cubes

8 baby carrots, cut into ½-inch-thick rounds

6 button mushrooms, quartered

1 small zucchini, quartered lengthwise and cut crosswise into ½-inch-thick pieces

1 cup bite-sized cauliflower florets

1 cup bite-sized broccoli florets

½ cup sliced water chestnuts

1 sheet purchased puff pastry

1 egg, lightly beaten

Preheat the oven to 400°F.

To make the sauce, combine all the ingredients except the cornstarch solution in a 2-quart saucepan. Place the pan over medium-high heat and bring to a boil, stirring constantly. Add the cornstarch solution and cook until the sauce thickens slightly, about 30 seconds. Remove from the heat and set aside.

Place a stir-fry pan over high heat until hot. Add the oil, swirling to coat the sides. Add the garlic and ginger and cook, stirring, until fragrant, about 15 seconds. Add the chicken and stir-fry for 1 minute. Add all the vegetables and stir-fry, adding a few drops of water if the pan appears dry, until the cauliflower is almost tender, about 3 minutes.

Spoon the chicken mixture into four 1½- to 2-cup ovenproof soup bowls. Pour one-fourth of the curry mixture into each bowl.

On a lightly floured surface, roll out the puff pastry ¼ inch thick and cut into 4 circles, each about ½ inch larger in diameter than the bowls. Top each bowl with a circle of pastry and press to seal the edges. Cut a 1-inch-long slit in center of each pastry and brush with the egg. Place the bowls in a baking pan and bake until the pastry is golden brown, 10 to 12 minutes. Remove from the oven and serve.

VIETNAMESE EGG CUSTARD

The combination of wood ears and bean thread noodles adds great texture to the gently steamed savory egg custard. Serve with Tangy Bean Sprout Salad (page 58) and Three-Minute Baby Bok Choy (page 172).

One 1½-ounce bundle dried bean thread noodles

2 dried wood ears

1 tablespoon vegetable oil

3 cloves garlic, minced

6 eggs

⅓ pound ground pork

⅓ cup chicken broth

1 teaspoon sugar

½ teaspoon salt

¼ teaspoon black pepper

¼ cup fresh cilantro leaves

2 red jalapeño chilies, thinly sliced

2 tablespoons soy sauce

In separate bowls, soak the bean thread noodles and the wood ears in warm water to cover until softened, about 10 minutes; drain. Cut the noodles into ½-inch lengths. Cut the wood ears into narrow strips. Set aside. Place a small frying pan over high heat until hot. Add the oil, swirling to coat the bottom. Add the garlic and cook, stirring, until fragrant, about 10 seconds. Set aside to cool. Prepare a stir-fry pan for steaming (see page 16). In a large bowl, lightly beat the eggs. Add the bean thread noodles, wood ears, garlic-oil mixture, pork, broth, sugar, salt, and pepper and mix well. Pour into a heat-proof glass pie dish.

Place the pie dish in the stir-fry pan, cover, and steam over medium heat until the eggs are set and the pork is cooked through, 8 to 10 minutes.

Remove the dish from the pan, top with the cilantro, chilies, and soy sauce, and serve.

MAKES 4 SERVINGS

SEAFOOD TRIO IN KUNG PAO SAUCE

This quick stir-fry is one of the most popular exports from the Chinese region of Sichuan, where chilies and peanuts are grown in abundance. Traditionally whole chilies are scraped and the paste is used to give the dish spice, but by substituting chili garlic sauce you can achieve the heat from the chilies without the sting. Look for frozen seafood combinations in the seafood case or freezer section of the supermarket.

MAKES 4 SERVINGS

1 pound **mixed seafood, such as shrimp, cleaned squid, and salmon fillet, or purchased premixed seafood,** thawed if frozen

1 teaspoon **cornstarch**

⅛ teaspoon **white pepper**

Sauce

2 tablespoons **Chinese black vinegar or balsamic vinegar**

2 tablespoons **soy sauce**

1½ tablespoons **hoisin sauce**

1 tablespoon **chili garlic sauce**

1 tablespoon **water**

2 teaspoons **sugar**

1 tablespoon **vegetable oil**

2 cloves **garlic,** minced

2 **green onions,** cut on the diagonal into ½-inch pieces

½ cup **sliced bamboo shoots**

½ cup **roasted peanuts**

Prepare the seafood: peel and devein the shrimp; cut the squid bodies crosswise into ½-inch-wide rings; remove the skin and any errant bones from the salmon and cut into bite-sized pieces. Place in a bowl, add the cornstarch and pepper, and stir to coat evenly. Set aside.

To make the sauce, combine all the ingredients in a small bowl and mix well.

Place a stir-fry pan over high heat until hot. Add the oil, swirling to coat the sides. Add the garlic and green onions and cook, stirring, until fragrant, about 30 seconds. Add the bamboo shoots and seafood and stir-fry until the seafood is opaque, 2 to 3 minutes; the length of time will depend on the seafood selected. Add the sauce and cook, stirring, until sauce boils and thickens slightly, about 30 seconds.

Transfer to a serving plate, sprinkle with the peanuts, and serve.

DINNER OYSTER OMELET

Here's a great way to use up all those extra eggs in the refrigerator. I use Chinese chives when they are in season; they have an almost garlicky flavor that intensifies when cooked. You can use regular chives or even the green portion of green onions in their place. Serve with Tangy Bean Sprout Salad (page 58) or a hearty soup like Beef Rice Soup (page 81).

MAKES 2 SERVINGS

One 10-ounce jar shucked oysters, drained
4 eggs
½ teaspoon cornstarch
¼ teaspoon salt
   Dash of white pepper
1 tablespoon vegetable oil
1 clove garlic, minced
½ cup bean sprouts
¼ cup shredded carrot
1 tablespoon chopped fresh Chinese chives
2 teaspoons chopped fresh cilantro
   Fresh cilantro sprigs for garnish
   Spicy Soy Dipping Sauce (page 34; optional)

Bring a small saucepan filled with water to a simmer over medium-high heat. Add the oysters and blanch for 1 minute; drain. Pat the oysters dry with paper towels and cut into bite-sized pieces.

In a bowl, whisk the eggs until blended. Add the cornstarch, salt, and pepper and whisk lightly to blend.

Place an 8- or 9-inch nonstick frying pan over medium heat until hot. Add the oil, swirling to coat the bottom. Add the garlic and cook, stirring, until fragrant, about 10 seconds. Pour the egg mixture into the pan. Sprinkle the oysters, bean sprouts, carrot, chives, and chopped cilantro evenly over the eggs. Cook, without stirring, until the edges begin to set, about 2 minutes, then lift with a spatula and shake or tilt the pan to let the egg flow beneath. Continue to cook until the egg no longer flows freely, about 2 minutes longer, then turn the omelet over and brown lightly on the other side.

Slide the omelet onto a serving plate. Garnish with the cilantro sprigs and serve with the dipping sauce, if desired.

STUFFED JUMBO GARLIC PRAWNS

Select the largest saltwater prawns—more accurately known as jumbo shrimp—available. This is a beautiful dish that can be served either as a main dish or as an appetizer. To save time, use a mini food processor to make the filling.

MAKES 4 SERVINGS

Filling

- 3 tablespoons minced garlic
- 1 green onion, minced
- 2 tablespoons vegetable oil
- 1 teaspoon chili garlic sauce
- 1 teaspoon fish sauce
- ½ teaspoon sesame oil
- ½ teaspoon salt
- ¼ teaspoon white pepper

- 16 jumbo prawns in the shell (about 1 pound)

To make the filling, combine all the ingredients in a small bowl and mix well.

Using kitchen scissors, cut the legs from the prawns, then cut through each shell along the underside of the shellfish to make a pocket. Fill each prawn with about 1 teaspoon of the filling. Arrange prawns in a heatproof dish. Prepare a stir-fry pan for steaming (see page 16). Place the dish in the stir-fry pan, cover, and steam the prawns over high heat until they turn pink, 5 to 6 minutes.

Remove the dish from the pan and serve the prawns in the shell.

CANTONESE SHRIMP SCRAMBLE

This home-style dish is popular in Cantonese kitchens. For a variation, I use fish sauce in place of the usual soy sauce, so feel free to use either. Cook the eggs to your preferred doneness. Serve as a quick meal with steamed rice, soup, or vegetables.

5 eggs
½ pound medium-sized raw shrimp, peeled and deveined
1 teaspoon cornstarch
½ teaspoon salt
½ teaspoon fish sauce
1 tablespoon vegetable oil
1 green onion, thinly sliced

MAKES 3 SERVINGS

In a bowl, beat the eggs with a fork until thoroughly blended but not frothy. Add the shrimp, cornstarch, salt, and fish sauce and mix well.

Place a non-stick frying pan over high heat until hot. Add the oil, swirling to coat the bottom. Add the egg mixture and cook undisturbed until the eggs are almost set, about 1 minute. Stir the eggs gently with a spoon and continue cooking until the shrimp begin to curl and turn pink and the eggs form creamy curds, about 2 minutes longer. Transfer to a serving plate, sprinkle with the green onion, and serve.

MONDAY-NIGHT DUMPLING SOUP

You can make this soup for a dinner for as few as 4 or as many as 20 people in just minutes. Look in the freezer section of your supermarket for frozen dumplings. Try a few different brands and choose your favorite.

MAKES 4 TO 6 SERVINGS

24 frozen potstickers, wontons, or other dumplings

1/2 pound medium-sized cooked, peeled shrimp

1 cup thinly sliced Quick Char Siu (page 169)

6 cups Quick Asian Chicken Broth (page 34) or purchased chicken broth

2 quarter-sized slices ginger, julienned

1 cup snow peas, cut in half on the diagonal

1/4 cup sliced bamboo shoots

1/2 teaspoon sesame oil

1/8 teaspoon white pepper

2 green onions, thinly sliced

Bring a large pot filled with water to a boil over high heat, add the dumplings, and cook according to the package directions. Drain, rinse with cold water, and drain again. Divide the dumplings among 4 to 6 soup bowls. Divide the shrimp and char siu evenly among the bowls.

Place the broth and ginger in the same large pot and bring to a boil over high heat. Add the snow peas, bamboo shoots, sesame oil, and pepper and cook for 1 minute.

Ladle the broth and vegetables into the bowls, dividing them evenly. Garnish with the green onions and serve.

SHRIMP AND SUGAR SNAP PEAS STIR-FRY

Prepare this simple dish for any night of the week. Try to keep a pound or two of frozen shrimp in your freezer for a quick meal. Most grocery stores sell sugar snap peas loose or in bags. The peas usually require no more than a quick rinse, as most do not have "strings."

Marinade

1	tablespoon minced ginger
2	teaspoons Chinese rice wine or dry sherry
2	teaspoons cornstarch
1	teaspoon red chili flakes
1	teaspoon sugar
¼	teaspoon salt
⅛	teaspoon white pepper

¾	pound medium-sized raw shrimp, peeled and deveined
1	tablespoon vegetable oil
½	yellow onion, thinly sliced
6	ounces sugar snap peas (about 2 cups)
¼	cup chicken broth
½	teaspoon sesame oil

To make the marinade, combine all the ingredients in a bowl and mix well. Add the shrimp and stir to coat evenly. Let stand for 10 minutes.

Place a stir-fry pan over high heat until hot. Add the oil, swirling to coat the sides. Add the onion and sugar snap peas and cook, stirring, until the peas are tender-crisp, about 2 minutes. Add the shrimp and stir-fry until they turn pink, about 1½ minutes. Add the broth and sesame oil and cook, stirring, until the broth boils and thickens slightly, about 20 seconds.

Transfer to a serving plate and serve.

MAKES 4 SERVINGS

HONEY-GARLIC GREEN TEA SHRIMP

Use a spice grinder to turn green tea leaves into a fine powder. If you don't have a grinder, use green tea in a bag. Cut the bags open and use the tea inside; most of the time it is pretty fragrant. You will be amazed at the subtle flavors the leaves impart in this dish.

MAKES 4 SERVINGS

Marinade

- 1 tablespoon cornstarch
- 2 teaspoons soy sauce

- 1 pound medium-sized raw shrimp, peeled and deveined

Sauce

- ⅓ cup chicken broth
- 2 tablespoons oyster-flavored sauce
- 1½ tablespoons honey
- ½ teaspoon sesame oil
- ½ teaspoon cornstarch

- 1 tablespoon vegetable oil
- 3 cloves garlic, minced
- 2 teaspoons ground green tea leaves
- ⅓ cup macadamia nuts

To make the marinade, combine the corn-starch and soy sauce in a bowl and mix well. Add the shrimp and stir to coat evenly. Let stand for 10 minutes.

To make the sauce, combine all the ingredients in a small bowl and stir until honey dissolves. Place a stir-fry pan over high heat until hot. Add the oil, swirling to coat the sides. Add the garlic and cook, stirring, until fragrant, about 10 seconds. Add the shrimp and stir-fry until they turn pink, 1½ to 2 minutes. Sprinkle the ground green tea over the shrimp and stir to coat evenly. Stir the sauce once, add to the pan, and bring to a boil. Reduce the heat to medium-low and cook, stirring, until the sauce thickens, 1 to 2 minutes.

Add the nuts, transfer to a plate, and serve.

SHRIMP IN LOBSTER SAUCE

Even though the name says lobster, you won't find any in this popular Chinese dish. The sauce combination was originally created for serving with lobster, but nowadays it is more often used with shrimp. Salted black beans, steamed small black soybeans fermented in salt traditionally used for this sauce, are only found in Asian markets and should be stored in an airtight container in a cool, dry place after opening. If you cannot find them, use black bean garlic sauce.

MAKES 4 SERVINGS

Marinade

- 1 tablespoon cornstarch
- 1 tablespoon Chinese rice wine or dry sherry
- 1/8 teaspoon white pepper

- 1 pound medium-sized raw shrimp, peeled and deveined
- 1/4 pound ground pork
- 2 teaspoons cornstarch

Sauce

- 1/4 cup chicken broth
- 3 tablespoons Chinese rice wine or dry sherry
- 2 teaspoons fish sauce
- 2 teaspoons sugar

- 1 tablespoon vegetable oil
- 1 tablespoon minced ginger
- 3 cloves garlic, minced
- 1 tablespoon salted black beans, rinsed and lightly crushed, **or 1½ teaspoons black bean garlic sauce**
- 2 green onions, cut into 2-inch lengths
- ½ yellow onion, diced
- 1 teaspoon cornstarch dissolved in 2 teaspoons water
- 1 egg, lightly beaten

To make the marinade, combine all the ingredients in a bowl and mix well. Add the shrimp and stir to coat evenly. Let stand for 10 minutes.

In another bowl, combine the pork and cornstarch and mix well. Set aside.

To make the sauce, combine all the ingredients in a small bowl and stir until the sugar dissolves.

Place a stir-fry pan over high heat until hot. Add the oil, swirling to coat the sides. Add the ginger, garlic, and black beans and cook, stirring, until fragrant, about 20 seconds. Add the pork and the green and yellow onions and cook until the meat is browned and crumbly, about 2 minutes. Add the shrimp and stir-fry until they begin to curl and turn pink, 1½ to 2 minutes. Add the sauce and bring to a boil. Add the cornstarch solution and cook, stirring, until the sauce boils and thickens, about 20 seconds. Stir in the egg and cook just until it begins to set, about 1 minute.

Transfer to a serving plate and serve.

SINGAPORE VELVET SHRIMP

A unique mix of spice flavors from the combination of chili sauce and curry powder caught the attention of my taste buds in Singapore. You'll have plenty of sauce, so serve with lots of steamed rice. Simply Gai Lan (page 182) or Almond Baby Bok Choy (page 177) makes a nice side dish.

Sauce

- ½ **cup ketchup**
- ½ **cup water**
- 2 **tablespoons sweet chili sauce**
- 1½ **tablespoons curry powder**

- 1 **tablespoon vegetable oil**
- 1 **lemongrass stalk,** bottom 4 inches only, minced
- 2 **cloves garlic,** minced
- 1 **teaspoon minced ginger**
- ½ **yellow onion,** thinly sliced
- ½ **red bell pepper,** seeded and thinly sliced
- 3 **green onions;** 2 cut into 2-inch pieces, 1 chopped
- 1 **pound medium-sized raw shrimp,** peeled and deveined
- 1 **tablespoon sesame oil**

MAKES 4 SERVINGS

To make the sauce, combine all the ingredients in a small bowl and mix well. Set aside. Place a stir-fry pan over high heat until hot. Add the oil, swirling to coat the sides. Add the lemongrass, garlic, and ginger and cook, stirring, until fragrant, about 15 seconds. Add the yellow onion, red bell pepper, and green onion pieces and stir-fry until the onion slices begin to brown on the edges, about 2 minutes. Add the shrimp and stir-fry until they begin to curl and turn pink, 1½ to 2 minutes. Add the sauce and cook, stirring, until the sauce boils and thickens slightly, about 30 seconds. Add the sesame oil and toss to coat the shrimp evenly.

Transfer to a plate, sprinkle with the chopped green onion, and serve.

SEA SCALLOPS IN SWEET CHILI SAUCE

I don't cook with sea scallops often, but when I do I always make a mental note to use them more frequently. These delicious, sweet white morsels of shellfish are hard not to like. You should find plenty of good-quality frozen scallops in the freezer section of your supermarket. To ensure that the frozen scallops retain their natural juices, thaw them in the refrigerator rather than at room temperature. Don't marinate for longer than 10 minutes, as the lime juice will begin to "cook" the raw scallops and the flesh will become mushy on the stove top. Serve with steamed rice.

Marinade

2 tablespoons fresh lime juice

1 tablespoon fish sauce

1 teaspoon grated ginger

1 pound sea scallops

2 tablespoons vegetable oil

¼ cup sweet chili sauce

2 tablespoons chicken broth

¼ cup chopped fresh cilantro

To make the marinade, combine all the ingredients in a bowl and mix well. Add the scallops and stir to coat evenly. Let stand for 10 minutes. Drain the scallops and pat dry with paper towels.

Heat a wide, nonstick frying pan over medium-high heat until hot. Add the oil, swirling to coat the bottom. When the oil is hot, add the scallops and panfry, turning once, until golden brown, about 2 minutes on each side. Meanwhile, in a small saucepan, combine the sweet chili sauce and broth. Bring to a simmer over medium-high heat and simmer until the sauce thickens slightly, about 2 minutes. Transfer the scallops to a serving plate. Drizzle with the chili sauce, garnish with the cilantro, and serve.

FIERY CHILI PEPPER SQUID

For quick cooking, purchase cleaned squid bodies or cleaned squid already sliced into rings. You will find them in the freezer section or at the seafood counter of the supermarket. If you want a somewhat milder dish, remove the seeds from the jalapeño chili. Serve with plenty of steamed rice to smother the fire!

MAKES 4 SERVINGS

1½   **pounds cleaned squid**

2   **teaspoons cornstarch**

Seasoning Salt

½   **teaspoon salt**

¼   **teaspoon Chinese five-spice powder**

⅛   **teaspoon cayenne pepper**

1   **tablespoon vegetable oil**

4   **cloves garlic,** minced

2   **tablespoons minced ginger**

1   **jalapeño chili,** thinly sliced into rings

2   **tablespoons chopped fresh cilantro**

Cut each squid body in half lengthwise. With a knife, lightly score the inside flesh in a crosshatch pattern. Place the tentacles and scored bodies in a bowl, sprinkle with the cornstarch, and stir to coat evenly. Set aside. To make the seasoning salt, combine all the ingredients in a small bowl and mix well. Measure out ¾ teaspoon and discard the remainder.

Place a stir-fry pan over high heat until hot. Add the oil, swirling to coat the sides. Add the garlic, ginger, and chili and cook, stirring, until fragrant, about 30 seconds. Add the squid and stir-fry until the edges of the squid begin to curl, 1 to 1½ minutes. Sprinkle the ¾ teaspoon seasoning salt over the squid and toss to coat evenly.

Transfer to serving plate, sprinkle with the cilantro, and serve.

WINE-STEAMED CLAMS

Try substituting your favorite dry white wine for the Chinese rice wine (and why not pour a glass for the chef while the clams are steaming?). Serve with a delicate soup, such as Tea-Flavored Chicken-Walnut Soup (page 79), and with Simple Sesame Noodles (page 204).

2 **pounds small hard-shell clams**

1 **lemon,** thinly sliced

4 **fresh cilantro sprigs**

1 **tablespoon minced ginger**

½ **cup chicken broth**

3 **tablespoons Chinese rice wine or dry sherry**

1 **tablespoon butter,** cut into bits

MAKES 4 SERVINGS

Scrub the clams under cold running water, and discard any with open shells that don't close when tapped.

Prepare a stir-fry pan for steaming (see page 16). Place the lemon slices and cilantro in a shallow, heatproof dish. Place the clams on top. Sprinkle the ginger, broth, and wine over the clams. Dot with the butter. Place the dish in the stir-fry pan, cover, and steam over high heat until the shells open, about 6 minutes. Transfer the clams to a serving plate; discard any unopened clams. Discard the lemon slices and cilantro. Pour the cooking liquid into a small bowl and serve with the clams.

OYSTERS IN PORT SAUCE

Shucked oysters packed in jars are convenient for making quick dinners. Here is a good tip: drain the oysters, rinse under cold water, then add a few teaspoons of cornstarch, mix them around together, and rinse again. This helps remove any hidden grit in the oysters. Young Asian chefs are beginning to incorporate Western ingredients into traditional Asian dishes. The port wine here is an excellent example.

MAKES 4 SERVINGS

Two 10-ounce jars shucked oysters, drained
1 tablespoon cornstarch
1 tablespoon vegetable oil
6 green onions, cut into 1-inch lengths
3 cloves garlic, thinly sliced
5 quarter-sized slices ginger, lightly crushed
1/3 cup port wine
1 tablespoon soy sauce
1 tablespoon oyster-flavored sauce
1 tablespoon cornstarch dissolved in 2 tablespoons water

In a colander, combine the oysters and cornstarch and mix lightly. Rinse under cold running water. Bring a saucepan filled with water to a boil over high heat. Add the oysters, parboil for 1 minute, and drain.

Place a 2-quart saucepan over high heat until hot. Add the oil, swirling to coat the bottom. Add the green onions, garlic, and ginger and cook, stirring, until the onions are fragrant and wilted, 30 to 40 seconds. Add the oysters, wine, soy sauce, and oyster-flavored sauce and bring to a boil. Reduce the heat to low, cover, and simmer until the sauce has reduced slightly, about 3 minutes. Add the cornstarch solution and cook, stirring, until the sauce boils and thickens, about 20 seconds. Transfer to a serving plate and serve.

BLACK PEPPER–BUTTER CRAB

There are two ways to prepare this recipe: start with a live crab, as I do, or buy one that is already cooked, cleaned, and cracked. The first method is quick if you live near a Chinese market where the butcher will kill, clean, and crack the live crab for you. The second method is even faster, however, because the crab has already been cooked once. You need to reheat it only briefly with the seasoning. Too much heat, and the meat will lose its sweet flavor.

Sauce

- ½ cup chicken broth
- ¼ cup Chinese rice wine or dry sherry
- 2 teaspoons fish sauce
- ¼ teaspoon black pepper

- 1 whole raw or cooked Dungeness crab, cleaned and cracked

   Cornstarch for dusting, if using raw crab
- 2 to 4 tablespoons vegetable oil
- 1 tablespoon butter
- 4 or 5 quarter-sized slices ginger, lightly crushed

MAKES 2 SERVINGS

To make the sauce, combine all the ingredients in a small bowl and mix well. Set aside.

If using raw crab, dust with cornstarch.

To cook the raw crab, place a stir-fry pan over high heat until hot. Add 4 tablespoons oil and the butter. When the butter melts, add the ginger and crab and cook, stirring, until the crab turns red, about 3 minutes. Add the sauce, mix well, reduce the heat to low, cover, and simmer for 4 minutes.

To prepare the cooked crab, place a stir-fry pan over high heat until hot. Add 2 tablespoons oil and the butter. When the butter melts, add the ginger and cook, stirring, until fragrant, about 30 seconds. Add the crab and stir-fry for 1 minute. Add the sauce and cook for 1 minute to heat through.

Place the crab and pan juices in a large bowl and serve. Use the pan juices for dipping.

MIRIN-GINGER CRAB

I've seen cooked stone crab claws in grocery-store seafood departments around the country. Purchasing these precooked claws makes preparing crab a snap. But if you have more time on your hands, you can use any type of live crab. Simply have the crab cleaned, then use it in place of the stone crab and cook it a bit longer. I serve this as an appetizer with the sauce as a dip, or over a bed of cooked rice noodles as a meal. It is delicious either way.

MAKES 4 SERVINGS

Sauce

½ cup chicken broth

¼ cup mirin

1 tablespoon black bean garlic sauce

1 teaspoon fish sauce

1 teaspoon soy sauce

1 tablespoon vegetable oil

1 tablespoon minced ginger

1½ pounds cooked stone crab claws

1 teaspoon cornstarch dissolved in
   1 tablespoon water

1 tablespoon chopped fresh basil

To make the sauce, combine all the ingredients in a small bowl and mix well.

Place a stir-fry pan over high heat until hot. Add the oil, swirling to coat the sides. Add the ginger and cook, stirring, until fragrant, about 15 seconds. Add the crab claws and sauce and stir to coat evenly. Cover the pan and cook for 2 to 3 minutes to heat the crab through. Lift the claws from the sauce and place on a serving plate.

Add the cornstarch solution to the pan and cook, stirring, until the sauce boils and thickens, about 30 seconds. Pour the sauce over the crab and sprinkle with the basil, or serve the sauce in a small bowl for dipping.

CANTONESE LOBSTER

The sweetness of lobster works well with the boldness of black bean garlic sauce, and the combination of salted black beans and ginger is uniquely Cantonese. You can make your own sauce, but I suggest that you purchase it premade in a jar. Start your meal with Back Country Mushroom-Daikon Soup (page 80) and accompany the lobster with Coconut Rice (page 196).

MAKES 4 SERVINGS

2 **lobster tails** (each about ½ pound)

Seasoning Mixture

4 **cloves garlic,** minced

2 **green onions,** cut into 1-inch lengths

1 **teaspoon minced ginger**

2 **teaspoons black bean garlic sauce**

1 **tablespoon vegetable oil**

⅓ **cup chicken broth**

¼ **cup Chinese rice wine or dry sherry**

2 **teaspoons cornstarch** dissolved in 1 tablespoon water

1 **teaspoon sesame oil**

1 **green onion,** julienned

Remove the lobster meat by cutting along the inner edges of the soft undershell. Using a fork, pry out the meat. Cut the meat into 1-inch pieces. Set aside.

To make the seasoning mixture, combine all the ingredients in a small bowl and mix well. Place a stir-fry pan over high heat until hot. Add the oil, swirling to coat the sides. Add the seasoning mixture and cook, stirring, until fragrant, about 30 seconds. Add the lobster meat and stir-fry until opaque, about 2 minutes. Add the broth and wine and bring to a boil. Add the cornstarch solution and cook, stirring, until the sauce boils and thickens, about 30 seconds. Stir in the sesame oil and green onion.

Transfer to a serving plate and serve.

BAKED BLACK-BEAN CATFISH

Farm-raised catfish can be found in nearly every supermarket. Purchase a little extra to use in Fish Fried Rice (page 192). Serve a fillet over a bed of Swiss Chard with Black Bean Garlic Sauce (page 183) and a small scoop of rice.

Marinade

2　tablespoons Chinese rice wine
　　or dry sherry
1　tablespoon black bean garlic sauce
1½　teaspoons sesame oil
1　teaspoon sugar

1　**pound catfish fillet,** cut into 4 equal pieces
1　**tablespoon vegetable oil**
½　**yellow onion,** thinly sliced

Preheat the oven to 350°F.

To make the marinade, combine all the ingredients in a bowl and mix well. Add the fish and turn to coat evenly. Let stand for 10 minutes.

Place a stir-fry pan over high heat until hot. Add the oil, swirling to coat the sides. Add the onion and stir-fry until the onion begins to brown on the edges, about 2 minutes. Spread the onion in an aluminum foil-lined rimmed baking sheet. Arrange the fish over the onion and drizzle with the remaining marinade.

Bake, uncovered, until the fish is opaque and just begins to flake, about 10 minutes.

Transfer to a serving plate and spoon any juices over the top.

MAKES 4 SERVINGS

POACHED HALIBUT OVER SOBA NOODLES

Jasmine pearl tea is quite special. Each little pearl is a tea leaf that has been hand rolled. This expensive tea can be found in fine tea shops and food stores. When brewed, the little pearl unfolds into a beautiful whole leaf. If you cannot locate this unique variety of tea, substitute 2 or 3 jasmine tea bags. All you need to complete an elegant menu for your next dinner party are Yan's Cocktail Nuts (page 42) and Ginger Sugar Snap Peas (page 178).

MAKES 4 SERVINGS

12 ounces dried soba noodles

Broth

4 cups water

¼ cup Chinese rice wine or dry sherry

¼ cup soy sauce

3 tablespoons jasmine pearls

4 quarter-sized slices ginger, lightly crushed

2 green onions, cut in half and lightly crushed

½ lime, sliced

2 teaspoons sugar

⅛ teaspoon white pepper

1 pound halibut fillet, cut into 4 equal pieces

2 tablespoons cornstarch dissolved in ¼ cup water

2 green onions, chopped

Bring a large pot filled with water to a boil over high heat. Add the noodles and cook according to the package directions. Drain, rinse with cold water, and drain again. Set aside.

To make the broth, combine all the ingredients in a deep frying pan with a lid and bring to a boil over high heat. Slide the fish into the broth, reduce the heat to medium, and simmer, uncovered, until the fish turns opaque and just begins to flake, 7 to 8 minutes. Remove the fish with a slotted spatula and place on a plate. Cover with aluminum foil, shiny side down, to keep warm.

Strain the broth and discard the solids. Return the broth to the pan and bring to a boil over high heat. Add the cornstarch solution and cook, stirring, until the sauce boils and thickens, about 1 minute. Reduce the heat to medium, add the noodles, and toss to coat evenly.

Lift out the noodles and divide among 4 shallow bowls. Top each bowl with a piece of fish. Pour any remaining sauce over the top. Garnish with the chopped green onions and serve.

STEAMED FISH WITH LEMONGRASS OIL

Steaming is a method used by most Chinese cooks. Here, I've blended two flavors, lemongrass and black pepper, I've enjoyed in Vietnam. Place the fish over the crushed lemongrass stalks, and a light citrus flavor is transferred to the fish.

Lemongrass Oil

- 3 **tablespoons vegetable oil**
- 1 **lemongrass stalk,** bottom 4 inches only, chopped

- 4 **dried black mushrooms**
- 1 ¼ **pounds firm white fish fillet such as cod or snapper,** about ¾ inch thick
- ¼ **teaspoon salt**
- ¼ **teaspoon black pepper**
- 2 **lemongrass stalks,** bottom 4 inches only, lightly crushed
- 2 **green onions,** julienned
- 2 **tablespoons minced ginger**

MAKES 4 SERVINGS

To make the lemongrass oil, place the oil in a small pan over high heat and heat until smoking. Remove from the heat and add the chopped lemongrass. Set aside.

In a small bowl, soak the mushrooms in warm water to cover until softened, about 15 minutes; drain. Discard the stems and thinly slice the caps.

Cut the fish crosswise into 4 equal pieces. Sprinkle the fish with the salt and pepper. Place the crushed lemongrass in the center of a shallow, heatproof dish. Lay the fish fillets on top. Sprinkle the mushrooms, green onions, and ginger over the fish.

Prepare a stir-fry pan for steaming (see page 16). Place the dish in the stir-fry pan, cover, and steam over high heat until the fish turns opaque and just begins to flake, 8 to 10 minutes. Remove the dish from the pan. Strain the lemongrass oil and reheat the oil to the smoking point. Pour the hot oil over the fish and serve.

FISH AND LONG BEAN STIR-FRY

Parboiling the long beans will cut down on the stir-frying time. You can also skip the step and just put the long beans in the wok before the fish, as they will take longer to cook. Serve with Coconut Squash Soup (page 70) and Fish Fried Rice (page 192).

MAKES 4 SERVINGS

Marinade

- 1 teaspoon vegetable oil
- 1 teaspoon cornstarch
- ⅛ teaspoon white pepper

- ¾ pound firm white fish fillet, such as halibut, cod, or grouper, thinly sliced

Sauce

- ⅓ cup chicken broth
- 2 tablespoons oyster-flavored sauce
- 1 tablespoon Chinese rice wine or dry sherry
- 1 teaspoon sugar

- ½ pound Chinese long beans, cut into 1-inch pieces
- 2 teaspoons vegetable oil
- ½ yellow onion, thinly sliced
- 2 teaspoons minced ginger
- 2 teaspoons cornstarch dissolved in 1 tablespoon water

To make the marinade, combine all the ingredients in a bowl and mix well. Add the fish and stir to coat evenly. Set aside.

To make the sauce, combine all the ingredients in a small bowl and mix well. Set aside.

Pour water to a depth of 2 inches into a saucepan and bring to a boil over high heat. Add the beans and cook until tender-crisp, about 3 minutes. Drain.

Place a stir-fry pan over high heat until hot. Add the oil, swirling to coat the sides. Add the onion and ginger and cook, stirring, until fragrant, about 30 seconds. Add the fish and stir-fry until it turns opaque, about 1½ minutes. Add the beans and the sauce and bring to a boil. Add the cornstarch solution and cook, stirring, until the sauce boils and thickens, about 20 seconds.

Transfer to a serving plate and serve.

STEAMED TOFU AND FISH

Here's a healthful dish with no added fat! Use your favorite fish. I like cod or halibut, but it also works nicely with salmon. Serve with Asian Cucumber Bisque (page 69) and Hue-Style Fried Rice (page 193).

MAKES 4 SERVINGS

3 dried black mushrooms

One-half 16-ounce package soft tofu, drained

1 pound firm white fish fillet such as cod or halibut, cut into 4 equal pieces

¼ cup sliced bamboo shoots

2 teaspoons minced ginger

½ teaspoon salt

¼ teaspoon white pepper

3 baby bok choy, cut lengthwise into quarters

Sauce

½ cup vegetable broth

2 tablespoons Chinese rice wine or dry sherry

1 teaspoon ground green tea leaves (see note, page 100)

1 teaspoon cornstarch

In a bowl, soak the mushrooms in warm water to cover until softened, about 15 minutes; drain. Discard the stems and cut each cap into 3 slices.

Prepare a stir-fry pan for steaming (see page 16). Cut the tofu into 4 equal pieces and place in a shallow, heatproof dish. Arrange the fish, mushrooms, and bamboo shoots over the tofu. Sprinkle with the ginger, salt, and pepper. Arrange the bok choy quarters around the edges of the fish. Place the dish in the stir-fry pan, cover, and steam over high heat until the fish turns opaque and just begins to flake, about 7 minutes.

While the fish is steaming, make the sauce. Combine all the ingredients in a small saucepan and place over medium-high heat. Bring to a boil and cook, stirring, until the sauce thickens slightly, about 20 seconds. Remove the dish from the pan, and pour the hot sauce over the fish. Serve at once.

SEARED MISO TUNA

When shopping for white miso—it will be in the refrigerated section with other tofu products—look for a light tan paste, rather than white. In other words, the name is misleading. For the best result for this dish, be sure to leave the raw ahi in thick chunks. Serve with Simply Gai Lan (page 182) and Soybean Fried Rice (page 190) for a complete meal.

Marinade

⅓ cup mirin

2 **green onions,** chopped

2 **tablespoons sesame seeds**

1 **pound sashimi-grade ahi tuna fillet,** cut into 4 equal pieces

Sauce

2 **tablespoons mirin**

2 **tablespoons white miso**

2 **teaspoons sugar**

2 **teaspoons grated ginger**

1 **tablespoon vegetable oil**

To make the marinade, combine all the ingredients in a bowl and mix well. Add the tuna and turn to coat evenly. Let stand for 10 minutes.

To make the sauce, combine all the ingredients in a small saucepan and stir until smooth. Place over low heat, bring to a simmer, and simmer for 2 minutes. Remove from the heat.

Place a nonstick frying pan over high heat until hot. Add the oil, swirling to coat the bottom. Remove the tuna from the marinade, place in the hot pan, and sear, turning once, until the fish is still pink and raw in the center but white on the edges, about 1½ minutes on each side.

Slice each portion across the grain, fan on a plate, and top with the warm sauce.

GRILLED SALMON SUSHI-RICE BOWL

This is a great one-bowl meal. The ingredient list looks long and hard to follow, but most of the items can be found in your Asian pantry or the Asian section of the supermarket. For dessert, prepare Tropical Fruit with Lemon-Ginger Syrup (page 212).

MAKES 4 SERVINGS

Sauce

1 tablespoon wasabi powder

2 tablespoons water

¾ cup Homemade Ponzu Sauce (page 36) or purchased *ponzu* sauce

¼ cup sake

2 tablespoons grated ginger

1 pound center-cut salmon fillet, cut into 4 equal pieces

¾ pound asparagus, ends trimmed

½ cup Homemade Ponzu Sauce (page 36) or purchased *ponzu* sauce

2 tablespoons vegetable oil

4 teaspoons sesame seeds

4 cups warm Sushi Rice (page 32)

2 teaspoons sesame oil

3 green onions, chopped

1 avocado, pitted, peeled, and cut into ½-inch cubes

1 English cucumber, cut into matchstick-sized strips

¼ cup sliced pickled ginger

To make the sauce, combine the wasabi powder and water in a saucepan and let bloom for 5 minutes. Add all the remaining ingredients and bring to a boil over high heat. Reduce the heat to medium-low and simmer until the sauce is reduced by half, about 10 minutes. Meanwhile, place the fish and asparagus in a large baking dish. Pour the ponzu sauce and oil over the fish and the asparagus and turn to coat evenly. Let stand for 10 minutes.

In a small frying pan, toast the sesame seeds over medium heat, shaking the pan frequently, until lightly colored, 3 to 4 minutes. Immediately pour onto a plate to cool.

Place a grill pan over medium heat until hot. Lift the asparagus from the marinade, place in the pan, and cook, turning occasionally, until tender-crisp, about 3 minutes. Transfer the asparagus to a plate and cover with aluminum foil, shiny side down, to keep warm. Lift the fish from the marinade and place in the grill pan. Cook, turning once, until it turns opaque and just begins to flake, 2 to 3 minutes on each side.

To serve, divide the rice among 4 bowls. Top with a piece of fish and some asparagus. Pour ¼ cup of the sauce over the fish in each bowl. Garnish each serving with the sesame oil, green onions, avocado, cucumber, pickled ginger, and sesame seeds.

PANFRIED SNAPPER WITH YAN'S SWEET-AND-SOUR SAUCE

Here, I've jazzed up store-bought sweet-and-sour sauce with a few additional ingredients. But if you are short on time, you can use the sauce straight from the bottle. Serve with a bowl of piping-hot steamed rice and some stir-fried vegetables.

MAKES 4 SERVINGS

Sauce

- 2 teaspoons vegetable oil
- ½ yellow onion, finely chopped
- 2 cloves garlic, minced
- 1 jalapeño chili, minced
- ½ red bell pepper, seeded and finely chopped
- 1 cup purchased sweet-and-sour sauce
- ⅓ cup chicken broth
- Salt
- White pepper

- All-purpose flour for dusting
- 1 egg
- 1½ pounds snapper fillet, cut into 4 equal pieces
- 2 tablespoons vegetable oil

To make the sauce, place a small saucepan over high heat until hot. Add the oil, swirling to coat the bottom. Add the onion, garlic, chili, and bell pepper and cook, stirring, until the vegetables are tender, 1½ to 2 minutes. Add the sweet-and-sour sauce, broth, and salt and pepper to taste and bring to a boil. Remove from the heat and cover to keep warm while the fish cooks.

Place flour in one bowl, and lightly beat the egg in another bowl. One at a time, dust the fish pieces with the flour, shaking off the excess. Then dip in the egg, drain briefly, and dust again with the flour.

Place a frying pan over medium-high heat until hot. Add the oil, swirling to coat the bottom. Place the fish in the pan and cook, turning once, until golden brown on both sides and opaque in the center, 4 to 5 minutes on each side.

Pour the warm sauce onto a large serving plate, place the fish on the sauce, and serve.

POACHED TROUT WITH TANGY SAUCE

I serve this dish during Chinese New Year because whole fish symbolizes prosperity for the entire year. Whole trout is available at most supermarkets, or you can use any mild fish you like. Estimate a little over ½ pound per person when purchasing your fish. Don't be intimidated by the idea of cooking a whole fish. They are very easy to cook. I cut along either side of the backbone to ensure even cooking.

1 **whole cleaned trout (about 1½ pounds)**
2 **green onions,** cut in half and lightly crushed
5 **quarter-sized slices ginger,** lightly crushed

Sauce

¼ **cup Chinese rice wine or dry sherry**
¼ **cup rice vinegar**
2 **tablespoons soy sauce**
1 **tablespoon fish sauce**
1 **tablespoon shredded ginger**
1 **green onion,** julienned

2 **teaspoons cornstarch** dissolved in
   1 tablespoon water

Place the fish on a cutting board and make 2 cuts, each ½ inch deep, along either side of the backbone, running each of them the length of the fish.

Pour water to a depth of 2 inches into a pan wide enough to hold the fish. Add the green onions and ginger and bring to a boil over high heat. Slide the fish into the water, reduce the heat to medium-low, cover, and simmer until the fish turns opaque and just begins to flake, 8 to 10 minutes.

While the fish is cooking, make the sauce. Combine all the ingredients in a small saucepan. Bring to a boil over medium-high heat, add the cornstarch solution, and cook, stirring, until the sauce thickens slightly, about 1 minute. Remove from the heat and keep warm.

With a slotted spatula, remove the fish from the poaching liquid and place on a serving plate. Pour the sauce over the fish and serve.

TEA-SMOKED SALMON

Serve this tasty fish hot or at room temperature. It's important to use an aluminum foil–lined pan and lid. Otherwise, you will spend more time scrubbing away the remnants of the smoking, than you will enjoying your meal. Serve with Spicy Soba Noodles (page 200) and Ginger Sugar Snap Peas (page 178) for dinner, or over Wo Ti's Garlicky Romaine Salad (page 64) for lunch or a light dinner.

MAKES 3 SERVINGS

Marinade

¼ cup soy sauce

¼ cup Chinese rice wine or dry sherry

1 tablespoon minced ginger

2 teaspoons sugar

1 **pound salmon fillet,** cut crosswise into 1-inch-wide pieces

Smoking Mixture

½ cup packed brown sugar

⅓ cup raw long-grain rice

¼ cup black or oolong tea leaves

2 whole star anise

½ **teaspoon cornstarch** dissolved in 2 teaspoons water

To make the marinade, combine all the ingredients in a bowl and mix well. Add the salmon and turn to coat evenly. Let stand for 10 minutes.

Line a stir-fry pan or frying pan and the inside of the pan lid with aluminum foil. Combine all the ingredients for the smoking mixture, spread in the pan, and set a round cake rack over. Remove the fish from the marinade and place on the rack. If you will be serving the fish hot, pour the marinade into a small saucepan and set aside. If serving at room temperature, discard the marinade. Place the stir-fry pan, uncovered, over high heat. When the mixture begins to smoke, cover the pan, reduce the heat to medium-low, and smoke until the salmon turns a rich, deep color, about 10 minutes. Turn off the heat and let stand, covered, for at least 5 minutes longer before removing the lid.

If serving the fish hot, make a sauce by bringing the reserved marinade to a boil over high heat. Add the cornstarch solution and cook, stirring, until the mixture thickens, about 30 seconds. Remove from the heat.

Transfer the fish to a plate and, if serving hot, pour the sauce over it.

CITRUS TURKEY STIR-FRY

Here's a stir-fry your family will gobble up. Most grocery stores carry a wide selection of turkey products: ground, cutlets, strips, and whole breasts. Use what is available, except for the ground meat. And remember to zest the orange before you segment it.

Marinade

- 1 tablespoon oyster-flavored sauce
- 2 teaspoons Chinese rice wine or dry sherry
- 1 teaspoon cornstarch

- 3/4 pound turkey breast strips or turkey cutlets
- 2 oranges

Sauce

- 3/4 cup fresh orange juice
- 1 tablespoon honey
- 2 teaspoons cornstarch
- 1/2 teaspoon sesame oil

- 1 tablespoon vegetable oil
- 2 teaspoons minced ginger
- 2 green onions, cut into 2-inch lengths
- 1/2 cup dried cranberries or dried cherries
- 6 ears baby corn, cut in half on the diagonal

MAKES 4 SERVINGS

To make the marinade, combine all the ingredients in a bowl and mix well. If using turkey cutlets, cut crosswise into strips 1/2 inch wide and 2 inches long. Place the strips in the marinade and stir to coat well. Let stand for 10 minutes.

Grate the zest from 1 orange; set aside. Segment both oranges (see page 16) and set the segments aside.

To make the sauce, combine all the ingredients in a bowl and stir until the honey dissolves. Place a stir-fry pan over high heat until hot. Add the oil, swirling to coat the sides. Add the ginger and green onions and cook, stirring, until fragrant, about 20 seconds. Add the turkey and stir-fry until no longer pink, about 2 minutes. Add the cranberries, corn, and the sauce and cook, stirring, for 2 minutes. Remove the pan from the heat.

Stir in the orange zest and orange segments, transfer to a plate, and serve.

GREAT WALL HOISIN PIZZA

Premade pizza crusts make this meal a snap. Use Quick Char Siu (page 169) or store-bought roasted chicken for topping. Serve with Wo Ti's Garlicky Romaine Salad (page 64) and Tropical Fruit with Lemon-Ginger Syrup (page 212).

MAKES 2 PIZZAS

Pizza Sauce

- ¼ cup hoisin sauce
- ¼ cup tomato paste
- 1 teaspoon sesame oil
- 1 teaspoon grated ginger

- 1½ cups sliced Quick Char Siu (page 169) or shredded roasted chicken
- 1 tablespoon hoisin sauce
- ½ teaspoon sesame oil
- ⅛ teaspoon Chinese five-spice powder

- Two 9-inch cooked pizza crusts
- 3 fresh shiitake mushrooms, stems discarded and caps thinly sliced
- ½ red bell pepper, seeded and thinly sliced
- ¼ cup chopped fresh cilantro

- 1 cup shredded mozzarella cheese (¼ pound)

Preheat the oven to 400°F.

To make the pizza sauce, combine all the ingredients in a small bowl and mix well. Set aside.

In a bowl, combine the pork, hoisin sauce, sesame oil, and five-spice powder. Stir to coat the pork evenly.

Spread half of the pizza sauce on each crust. Top each with half of the mushrooms, bell pepper, meat, and cilantro. Sprinkle half of the cheese over each pizza.

Place the topped crusts on an aluminum foil–lined rimmed baking sheet. Bake until the cheese is bubbly, about 10 minutes.

Transfer the pizzas to a cutting board, cut into wedges, and serve.

GINGER CHICKEN

Here's my version of a dish my mom used to make when I was growing up. There are only a few ingredients, but the dish is very tasty. Make sure to wash the ginger root before using it, because you won't need to peel it for this recipe. Don't eat the ginger; its role is to flavor the oil. Serve with Carrot-Pineapple Rice (page 197).

MAKES 4 SERVINGS

Marinade

- 1 tablespoon cornstarch
- 1 tablespoon Chinese rice wine or dry sherry
- 1 teaspoon regular soy sauce
- 1 teaspoon dark soy sauce

- 1 pound boneless, skinless chicken thigh meat, cut into 1/2-inch cubes
- 2 tablespoons vegetable oil
- 1/3 cup thickly sliced ginger
- 1/2 cup chicken broth
- 1/2 cup pineapple chunks
- 2 teaspoons sliced pickled ginger

To make the marinade, combine all the ingredients in a bowl and mix well. Add the chicken and stir to coat evenly. Let stand for 10 minutes.

Place a stir-fry pan over high heat until hot. Add the oil, swirling to coat the sides. Add the fresh ginger and cook, stirring, until the ginger is crispy and the oil is infused with its flavor, about $1\frac{1}{2}$ minutes. Add the chicken and stir-fry until it is no longer pink in the center, 3 to 4 minutes. Add the broth and pineapple and cook, stirring, until the sauce boils and thickens slightly, about 20 seconds. Transfer to a serving plate, garnish with the pickled ginger, and serve.

SAVORY JADE CHICKEN

The texture and flavor contrast between the fried and fresh mint is simply delicious. This recipe does not use much oil, and it is super-quick.

Marinade

- 1 tablespoon soy sauce
- 2 teaspoons cornstarch

- 1 pound boneless, skinless chicken breast or thigh meat, cut into 1-inch pieces
- ¼ cup vegetable oil
- ¾ cup lightly packed fresh mint leaves
- 1 red jalapeño chili, thinly sliced
- ¼ cup Chinese rice wine or dry sherry
- 1 tablespoon chili garlic sauce
- 2 teaspoons sesame oil

To make the marinade, combine the soy sauce and cornstarch in a bowl and mix well. Add the chicken and stir to coat evenly. Let stand for 10 minutes.

Place a stir-fry pan over high heat. Add the vegetable oil and heat to almost smoking. Add ½ cup of the mint leaves and cook until the leaves are crisp, about 30 seconds. Remove with a slotted spoon and drain on paper towels. Set aside for garnish.

Remove all but 1 tablespoon of the oil from the pan and return the pan to the heat. Add the chicken and chili and stir-fry until the chicken is no longer pink in the center, 3 to 4 minutes. Add the wine and chili garlic sauce and cook for 30 seconds. Add the sesame oil and the remaining ¼ cup fresh mint leaves, remove the pan from the heat, and toss to coat.

Transfer to a serving platter, garnish with the fried mint, and serve.

MANGO-MACADAMIA CHICKEN

I've combined two ingredients that bring back fond memories of Hawaii: mangoes and macadamia nuts. They are quickly stir-fried with chicken and a bit of fish sauce and lemon juice, resulting in a delicious dish that will brighten any dinner table.

MAKES 4 SERVINGS

Marinade

2 teaspoons cornstarch

1 teaspoon soy sauce

¾ **pound boneless, skinless chicken breast or thigh meat,** cut into ½-inch cubes

Sauce

⅓ cup chicken broth

1 tablespoon fresh lemon juice

2 teaspoons fish sauce

1½ teaspoons sugar

---

2 teaspoons vegetable oil

2 **cloves garlic,** minced

½ teaspoon red chili flakes

1 **teaspoon cornstarch** dissolved in 1 tablespoon water

---

1 **small mango,** peeled, pitted, and cut into cubes

⅓ **cup chopped macadamia nuts**

To make the marinade, combine the cornstarch and soy sauce in a bowl and mix well. Add the chicken and stir to coat evenly. Let stand for 10 minutes.

To make the sauce, combine all the ingredients in a small bowl and stir until the sugar dissolves.

Place a stir-fry pan over high heat until hot. Add the oil, swirling to coat the sides. Add the garlic and red chili flakes and cook, stirring, until fragrant, about 15 seconds. Add the chicken and stir-fry until it is no longer pink in the center, 3 to 4 minutes. Add the sauce and bring to a boil. Add the cornstarch solution and cook, stirring, until the sauce boils and thickens, about 30 seconds. Add the mango and toss to coat with sauce.

Transfer the chicken to a serving plate, sprinkle with the nuts, and serve.

ORANGE PEEL CHICKEN

Chinese cooks typically use dried tangerine peel for this dish, but I've created a recipe utilizing something easily found in most markets: oranges. I use my knife to remove the peel from the orange, but a sharp vegetable peeler will also make quick work of the job. To reduce the bitterness of the orange peel, remove all the white pith, leaving only the colored portion, or zest.

Marinade

- 2   teaspoons soy sauce
- 1   teaspoon cornstarch

- 1   **pound boneless, skinless chicken breast or thigh meat,** cut into 1-inch cubes

Sauce

- ⅓   cup fresh orange juice
- 2   tablespoons Chinese rice wine or dry sherry
- 1   tablespoon hoisin sauce
- 2   teaspoons sugar
- 1   teaspoon chili garlic sauce

- 1   tablespoon vegetable oil
- 3   **green onions,** cut into 2-inch lengths
      Peel of 1 orange, cut into narrow strips 2 inches long
- 2   **teaspoons cornstarch** dissolved in 1 tablespoon water

To make the marinade, combine the soy sauce and cornstarch and mix well. Add the chicken and stir to coat evenly. Let stand for 10 minutes. To make the sauce, combine all the ingredients in a small bowl and stir until the sugar dissolves.

Place a stir-fry pan over high heat until hot. Add the oil, swirling to coat the sides. Add the chicken, green onions, and half of the orange peel. Stir-fry until the chicken is no longer pink in the center, 3 to 4 minutes. Add the sauce and bring to a boil. Add the cornstarch solution and cook, stirring, until the sauce boils and thickens, about 30 seconds. Add the remaining orange peel and stir to coat evenly.

Transfer to a serving plate and serve.

CILANTRO CHICKEN

Sometimes when I want to wow my dinner guests, I'll cook using two woks, one for the chicken and the other for the vegetables. Then I toss the chicken and vegetables together just before serving. Because most of the cilantro flavor is in the stems and roots, using the cilantro stems with the leaves will intensify the flavor.

MAKES 4 SERVINGS

Marinade

- 1 tablespoon soy sauce
- 2 teaspoons Chinese rice wine or dry sherry
- 2 teaspoons cornstarch
- ¾ teaspoon ground coriander
- 2 teaspoons minced ginger

- ¾ pound boneless, skinless chicken breast or thigh meat, cut into 1-inch cubes
- 1 tablespoon vegetable oil
- 1 walnut-sized shallot, cut into quarters
- 2 cups bean sprouts
- ½ cup shredded carrot
- ⅓ cup chopped fresh cilantro leaves and stems
- ⅓ cup pistachios

To make the marinade, combine all the ingredients in a bowl and mix well. Add the chicken and stir to coat evenly. Let stand for 10 minutes.

Place a stir-fry pan over high heat until hot. Add the oil, swirling to coat the sides. Add the shallot and cook, stirring, until fragrant, about 20 seconds. Add the chicken and stir-fry until it is no longer pink in the center, 3 to 4 minutes. Add the bean sprouts and carrot and cook, stirring, until the bean sprouts begin to wilt, about 1 minute. Add the cilantro and pistachios, stir well, and toss to coat.

Transfer to a serving plate and serve.

TANGY BLACK-PEPPER CHICKEN

If you can't find black pepper sauce in your market, you can make your own: combine 2 tablespoons oyster-flavored sauce and 1½ teaspoons black pepper, and get ready for a kick.

Marinade

- 2 teaspoons cornstarch
- ¼ teaspoon black pepper
- 1 teaspoon soy sauce

- ¾ pound boneless, skinless chicken breast or thigh meat, cut into ½-inch cubes
- 1 lemon
- 2 tablespoons black pepper sauce
- 1 tablespoon vegetable oil
- 2 cloves garlic, minced
- ½ yellow onion, diced
- 1 small red bell pepper, seeded and diced
- 1 small green bell pepper, seeded and diced

MAKES 4 SERVINGS

To make the marinade, combine all the ingredients in a bowl and mix well. Add the chicken and stir to coat evenly. Let stand for 10 minutes.

Grate the zest from the lemon, then squeeze the juice. Combine the zest, 2 tablespoons of the juice, and the black pepper sauce in a small bowl.

Place a stir-fry pan over high heat until hot. Add the oil, swirling to coat the sides. Add the garlic and onion and cook, stirring, until fragrant, about 30 seconds. Add the chicken and stir-fry until it is no longer pink in the center, about 3 minutes. Add the bell peppers and stir-fry until the peppers are tender-crisp, about 2 minutes. Add the black pepper–lemon mixture and toss to coat evenly.

Transfer to a serving plate and serve.

LEMONGRASS CHICKEN OVER RICE STICK NOODLES

Looks can be deceiving. Although the list of ingredients for this looks long, most of the items are in your Asian pantry, so you'll find everything quickly. This is a light dish that can be served in no time flat! If you don't have the noodles, serve it over steamed jasmine rice. If you have a mini food processor, coarsely chop the lemongrass on a cutting board and then give it a few pulses in the food processor to mince.

Marinade

- 1 **lemongrass stalk,** bottom 4 inches only, finely minced
- 1 **tablespoon soy sauce**
- 1 **teaspoon cornstarch**
- 1/4 **teaspoon black pepper**

- 3/4 **pound boneless, skinless chicken breast meat,** cut into 1-inch cubes
- 8 **ounces dried rice stick noodles**
- 1 **tablespoon vegetable oil**
- 2 **cloves garlic,** minced
- 2 **red jalapeño chilies,** seeded and julienned
- 1 1/2 **teaspoons sugar**
- 1/4 **cup chicken broth**
- 3 **green onions,** julienned
- 1 **tablespoon fish sauce**
- 1 **tablespoon fresh lemon juice**
- 3 **tablespoons chopped fresh mint**
- 1/2 **cup Southeast Asian All-Purpose Dipping Sauce (page 35)**

To make the marinade, combine all the ingredients in a bowl and mix well. Add the chicken and stir to coat evenly. Let stand for 10 minutes.

Bring a large pot filled with water to a boil over high heat. Add the noodles and cook until tender, about 3 minutes. Drain, rinse with cold water, and drain again. Set aside. Place a stir-fry pan over high heat until hot. Add the oil, swirling to coat the sides. Add the garlic, chilies, and sugar and cook, stirring, until the garlic is fragrant and the sugar begins to caramelize, about 15 seconds. Add the chicken and stir-fry until the surface of the chicken turns white, about 1 minute. Add the broth, reduce the heat to medium, cover, and cook until the chicken is no longer pink in the center, 3 to 4 minutes. Add the green onions, fish sauce, and lemon juice and cook for 30 seconds. Remove from the heat and stir in the mint.

Place the noodles on a serving plate and spoon the chicken mixture over the top. Serve the dipping sauce in a bowl alongside.

FRAGRANT CHICKEN

Frying the whole shallots and garlic until golden brown gives this dish a mildly nutty flavor. Use a small pan, so you won't need too much oil. Remember, however, you can refrigerate the oil and use it again. The shallots and garlic will have imparted a subtle flavor to it.

Marinade

- 1 tablespoon regular soy sauce
- 1 teaspoon dark soy sauce
- 2 teaspoons Chinese rice wine or dry sherry
- 2 teaspoons cornstarch

- 1 pound boneless, skinless chicken breast meat, cut into 1-inch cubes

Sauce

- ⅓ cup chicken broth
- 2 tablespoons Chinese rice wine or dry sherry
- 1 tablespoon oyster-flavored sauce
- ½ teaspoon black bean garlic sauce

- 1 cup vegetable oil
- 6 cloves garlic, peeled
- 3 small shallots, peeled
- 1 teaspoon cornstarch dissolved in 2 teaspoons water

To make the marinade, combine all the ingredients in a bowl and mix well. Add the chicken and stir to coat evenly. Let stand for 10 minutes.

To make the sauce, combine all the ingredients in a small bowl and mix well. Set aside. Pour the oil into a small saucepan and place over high heat. When the surface of the oil begins to shimmer, add the garlic and shallots. Cook, stirring, until golden brown, about 1 minute. Remove with a slotted spoon and drain on paper towels. Remove the oil from the heat.

Place a stir-fry pan over high heat until hot. Add 1 tablespoon of the garlic-shallot oil, swirling to coat the sides. Add the chicken and stir-fry until it is no longer pink in the center, 3 to 4 minutes. Add the browned shallots and garlic and the sauce and bring to a boil. Add the cornstarch solution and cook, stirring, until the sauce boils and thickens, about 45 seconds.

Transfer to a serving plate and serve.

BRAISED CHICKEN AND TARO

A delicious one-pot meal that's perfect for a cold winter night. Cook this on the weekend and have leftovers for later in the week. Chinese sausage is only found in Asian markets, and there is no other sausage with a similar flavor. If you can't locate it, omit the sausage from the recipe.

6 **dried black mushrooms**

1 **pound boneless, skinless chicken thigh meat,** cut into 1-inch cubes

2 **tablespoons cornstarch**

Sauce

1 **cup chicken broth**

¼ **cup Chinese rice wine or dry sherry**

3 **tablespoons soy sauce**

¼ **teaspoon white pepper**

1 **tablespoon vegetable oil**

5 **cloves garlic,** sliced

1 **tablespoon minced ginger**

2 **Chinese sausages (2 ounces each),** cut on the diagonal into ½-inch-thick slices

1 **pound taro,** peeled and cut into 1-inch cubes

2 **green onions,** cut into 1½-inch pieces

In a bowl, soak the mushrooms in warm water to cover until softened, about 15 minutes; drain. Discard the stems and cut the caps in half.

In a bowl, combine the chicken and cornstarch and turn to coat the chicken evenly. Let stand for 10 minutes.

To make the sauce, combine all the ingredients in a small bowl and mix well.

Place a 3-quart saucepan over high heat until hot. Add the oil, swirling to coat the bottom. Add the garlic and ginger and cook, stirring, until fragrant, about 15 seconds. Add the chicken and sausages and stir-fry until the chicken is lightly browned, 2 to 3 minutes. Add the mushrooms, taro, green onions, and sauce, reduce the heat to medium-low, cover, and simmer, stirring occasionally, until the taro is tender, about 15 minutes.

Transfer to a serving bowl and serve.

THREE-ALARM FIRECRACKER CHICKEN

A jalapeño chili, dried red chilies, and chili garlic sauce—that's what I call a hot and spicy dish. In China, the dried chilies are eaten with the chicken, but unless you like very hot food, you should set them aside.

MAKES 4 SERVINGS

Marinade

2 teaspoons regular soy sauce

1 teaspoon dark soy sauce

1 teaspoon cornstarch

1 pound boneless, skinless chicken breast meat, cut crosswise into ½-inch-wide strips

Sauce

⅓ cup ketchup

¼ cup chicken broth

1 tablespoon chili garlic sauce

1 teaspoon sugar

1 tablespoon vegetable oil

1 jalapeño chili, cut into narrow strips

8 small dried red chilies

1 red bell pepper, seeded and cut into narrow strips

½ yellow onion, thinly sliced

To make the marinade, combine all the ingredients in a bowl and mix well. Add the chicken and stir to coat evenly. Let stand for 10 minutes.

To make the sauce, combine all the ingredients in a small bowl and mix well.

Place a stir-fry pan over high heat until hot. Add the oil, swirling to coat the sides. Add the jalapeño and dried chilies and cook, stirring, until the dried chilies begin to brown, about 15 seconds. Add the chicken, bell pepper, and onion and stir-fry until the chicken is no longer pink in the center, 2 to 3 minutes. Add the sauce, bring to a boil, and stir to coat the chicken evenly.

Transfer to a serving plate and serve.

RICE COOKER CHICKEN AND MUSHROOMS

A rice cooker can be used to cook a variety of dishes, from soups to this one-dish meal. The most versatile rice cooker holds about 10 cups, a size that allows you to make a variety of different dishes. As each rice cooker is different, test the doneness of the chicken once the cooking cycle finishes to ensure it is cooked completely.

MAKES 4 SERVINGS

6 **dried black mushrooms**

½ **pound boneless, skinless chicken thigh meat,** cut into 1-inch cubes

2 **tablespoons oyster-flavored sauce**

1 **tablespoon Chinese rice wine or dry sherry**

¼ **teaspoon Chinese five-spice powder**

2 **teaspoons minced ginger**

1½ **cups raw long-grain rice**

2¾ **cups chicken broth**

2 **green onions,** thinly sliced

In a bowl, soak the mushrooms in warm water to cover until softened, about 15 minutes; drain. Discard the stems and quarter the caps. In a bowl, combine the chicken, oyster-flavored sauce, wine, five-spice powder, and ginger and mix well.

Place the chicken in a rice cooker. Add the mushrooms, rice, and broth and stir to mix. Cook according to the manufacturer's instructions.

When the rice and chicken are done, sprinkle with the green onions and serve.

GRILLED SATAY CHICKEN TENDERS

You can use boneless chicken thighs or breasts for this recipe, but when time is short, try chicken breast tenders. Also called tenderloins, they are cut from the bottom of the chicken breast and, as their name implies, they are, well, tender. I like to serve the satay with the Garlicky Peanut Noodles (page 208).

Marinade

2	tablespoons soy sauce
2	tablespoons fresh lemon juice
2	tablespoons curry powder
1	tablespoon packed brown sugar
1	tablespoon vegetable oil
½	teaspoon ground cumin
¼	teaspoon Chinese five-spice powder

1	pound chicken breast tenders

To make the marinade, combine all the ingredients in a bowl and mix well. Add the chicken and stir to coat evenly. Let stand for 10 minutes.

Place a grill pan over medium-high heat until hot. Remove the chicken from the marinade and pour the marinade into a small saucepan. Place the chicken on the grill pan and cook, turning once, until it is no longer pink in the center, about 2 minutes on each side. Meanwhile, place the marinade over medium-high heat and bring to a simmer.

Transfer the chicken to a serving plate, pour the sauce over the top, and serve.

MAKES 4 SERVINGS

CHICKEN AND POTATO YELLOW CURRY

With great premade curries on most grocery-store shelves, this recipe is a must for any quick and easy kitchen. If you are in a huge hurry, use canned potatoes, which will eliminate one step. Make a double batch of the curry; the flavor only gets better the next day.

MAKES 4 TO 6 SERVINGS

3 **thin-skinned potatoes (about 1 ¼ pounds total weight),** unpeeled and cut into quarters

One **13½-ounce can unsweetened coconut milk**

3 **tablespoons yellow curry paste**

⅓ **cup water**

1 **pound boneless, skinless chicken breast or thigh meat,** cut into 1-inch cubes

3 **tablespoons sugar**

3 **tablespoons fish sauce**

¼ **cup chopped fresh cilantro**

1 **teaspoon cornstarch** dissolved in 2 teaspoons water

Fresh cilantro leaves for garnish

In a saucepan, cook the potatoes in boiling water to cover until tender, about 15 minutes; drain.

Pour ½ cup of the coconut milk into a saucepan and place over medium heat for 30 seconds. Stir in the curry paste and bring slowly to a boil, stirring constantly. Add the remaining coconut milk and the water and bring to a boil. Add the chicken and cook, stirring occasionally, until it is no longer pink in the center, 3 to 4 minutes. Add the sugar, fish sauce, and potatoes, bring to a boil, and cook for 5 minutes. Add the chopped cilantro and the cornstarch solution and cook, stirring, until the sauce boils and thickens slightly, about 1 minute.

Transfer to a serving plate, garnish with the cilantro leaves, and serve.

SWEET SOY-BRAISED CHICKEN DRUMMETTES

Most supermarkets carry the little drummettes that come from whole chicken wings. You can also use regular drumsticks, but you need to cook them longer. Serve with a bowl of steamed rice and pass a small bowl of some of the braising liquid alongside.

2	cups water
½	cup dark soy sauce
⅓	cup regular soy sauce
⅓	cup packed brown sugar
4	quarter-sized slices ginger, lightly crushed
2	green onions, chopped
1	whole star anise
⅛	teaspoon Chinese five-spice powder
1½	to 2 pounds chicken wing drummettes

In a 3-quart saucepan, combine the water, soy sauces, brown sugar, ginger, green onions, star anise, and five-spice powder and mix well. Add the chicken and bring to a boil over high heat. Reduce the heat to medium, cover, and simmer, stirring occasionally, until the chicken is tender, 20 to 25 minutes. Remove the chicken with a slotted spoon, place on a serving plate, and serve.

If you wish, let the braising liquid cool, then cover and refrigerate. You can use it again by adding a little more water and soy sauce.

MAKES 4 TO 6 SERVINGS

DUCK BREAST À L'ORANGE, ASIAN STYLE

On elegant French menus, you'll often find duck à l'orange, a whole roasted duck with a tasty orange-brandy glaze. I've found that orange and Chinese five-spice powder are a delicious combination, so I've made an Asian version of this French classic. I like to sear the whole duck breast to medium-rare, but you can instead slice and stir-fry the meat.

MAKES 4 SERVINGS

Marinade

- 1 tablespoon fish sauce
- 1 teaspoon cornstarch
- ⅛ teaspoon salt

- 1 **pound boneless duck breasts,** skin scored

Sauce

- ½ cup fresh orange juice
- 1 tablespoon minced ginger
- 1 teaspoon chili garlic sauce
- ⅛ teaspoon Chinese five-spice powder

- 2 **oranges,** segmented **(see page 16)**
- 1 tablespoon coarsely chopped crystallized ginger (optional)

Preheat the oven to 375°F.

To make the marinade, combine all the ingredients in a bowl and mix well. Add the duck and turn to coat evenly. Let stand for 10 minutes.

To make the sauce, combine all the ingredients in a small saucepan. Set aside.

Place a nonstick, ovenproof frying pan over high heat until hot. Place the duck, skin side down, in the pan and cook until golden brown, about 3 minutes. Turn the breasts over and cook for 3 minutes longer. Place the pan in the oven and roast until the duck is medium-rare, 8 to 10 minutes. Remove from the oven and let the duck rest for 5 minutes. Do not cover the duck or the skin will not be crisp.

While the duck is resting, bring the sauce to a boil over medium-high heat. Cook until it reduces slightly, about 2 minutes. Remove from the heat, add the orange segments, and stir to coat.

Slice the duck and arrange on a serving plate. Pour the sauce over the duck and sprinkle with the crystallized ginger, if desired.

SEARED FIVE-SPICE DUCK BREAST WITH SNOW PEAS AND WATERCRESS

Don't be surprised to see watercress used here. The nutty-flavored green grows in abundance in the wetlands of China. Watercress has a peppery flavor that will add a nice zing to this dish. Serve as a main course for lunch or as a starter for an elegant dinner.

Dressing

- 3 tablespoons rice vinegar
- 2 tablespoons vegetable oil
- 1 tablespoon soy sauce
- 2 teaspoons sesame oil
- 1 tablespoon grated ginger
- 1 teaspoon sugar
- ½ teaspoon salt

- 1 teaspoon salt
- ½ teaspoon Chinese five-spice powder
- ¾ pound boneless duck breasts, skin scored

- 1 bunch watercress (¼ pound), tough stems removed
- 2 cups snow peas, thinly sliced
- 2 cups shredded napa cabbage

To make the dressing, combine all the ingredients in a small bowl and mix well. Set aside. Combine the salt and five-spice powder and sprinkle the mixture over the duck.

Place a nonstick frying pan over high heat until hot. Place the duck, skin side down, in the pan and cook until golden brown, about 3 minutes. Turn the breasts, reduce the heat to medium, and cook until medium-rare, 6 to 7 minutes. Remove the duck from the pan, place on a cutting board, and let rest for 5 minutes. Do not cover the duck or the skin will not be crisp.

In a large bowl, combine the watercress, snow peas, and cabbage. Pour the dressing over the top and toss to coat. Divide the salad among 4 serving plates. Cut the duck into slices on the diagonal. Arrange the slices on each salad and serve.

STIR-FRIED BEEF AND SPINACH SALAD

Is it a stir-fry or a salad? You decide. No matter which it is, yin and yang are in perfect harmony: the contrasting cool spinach and hot beef stir-fry tossed together. The slightly wilted spinach still retains a fresh taste. Perfect for a light dinner, or serve with some steamed rice and a tofu dish for the entire family.

MAKES 4 SERVINGS

Marinade

- 2 tablespoons soy sauce
- 2 teaspoons cornstarch

- ¾ **pound flank steak,** thinly sliced across the grain

Sauce

- ¼ cup chicken broth
- 2 tablespoons rice vinegar
- 1 tablespoon soy sauce
- 1 tablespoon oyster-flavored sauce
- 1 tablespoon sweet chili sauce
- 2 teaspoons sugar
- ¼ teaspoon sesame oil

- 1½ tablespoons vegetable oil
- 1 **clove garlic,** chopped
- 1 **yellow onion,** thinly sliced
- 1 **red bell pepper,** seeded and thinly sliced
- ½ **pound baby spinach (about 6 cups)**

To make the marinade, combine the soy sauce and cornstarch and mix well. Add the beef and stir to coat evenly. Let stand for 10 minutes.

To make the sauce, combine all the ingredients in a small bowl and stir until the sugar dissolves. Set aside.

Place a stir-fry pan over high heat until hot. Add 1 tablespoon of the oil, swirling to coat the sides. Add the garlic and cook, stirring, until fragrant, about 10 seconds. Add the beef and stir-fry until it is no longer pink in the center, 2 to 3 minutes. Remove the meat from the pan.

Add the remaining ½ tablespoon oil to the pan. Add the onion and bell pepper and cook, stirring, until the onion is tender and begins to brown on the edges, about 2 minutes.

Pour the sauce into the pan and bring to a boil. Return the beef to the pan and cook for 1 minute to heat through. Remove the pan from the heat, add the spinach, and toss to coat with the sauce. Immediately transfer to a serving plate and serve.

TROPICAL BEEF

This is an interesting combination of garden vegetables and sweet and tangy fruit. I tasted a similar dish at a local Thai restaurant, and it inspired me to create this variation. Cucumbers can be added to any stir-fry. They don't always need to be eaten cold with dips or in salads. It's easy to remove the seeds: slice the cucumber in half lengthwise and use a spoon to scoop them out.

Marinade

¼   **cup pineapple juice**

1   **tablespoon soy sauce**

1   **tablespoon cornstarch**

¾   **pound flank steak,** cut into ½-inch cubes

Sauce

¼   **cup pineapple juice**

1   **tablespoon oyster-flavored sauce**

1   **tablespoon sweet chili sauce**

1   **tablespoon vegetable oil**

½   **cucumber,** peeled, seeded, and cut into ½-inch cubes

1   **plum tomato,** cut into ½-inch cubes

½   **yellow onion,** cubed

½   **cup pineapple chunks**

½   **mango,** peeled and cut into ½-inch cubes

1   **teaspoon cornstarch** dissolved in 1 tablespoon water

MAKES 4 SERVINGS

To make the marinade, combine all the ingredients in a bowl and mix well. Add the beef and stir to coat evenly. Let stand for 10 minutes.

To make the sauce, combine all the ingredients in a small bowl and mix well.

Place a stir-fry pan over high heat until hot. Add the oil, swirling to coat the sides. Add the beef and stir-fry until seared, about 1 minute. Add the cucumber, tomato, and onion and cook, stirring, until the cucumber is tender-crisp, about 1½ minutes. Add the pineapple, mango, and sauce and bring to a boil. Add the cornstarch solution and cook, stirring, until the sauce boils and thickens, about 20 seconds.

Transfer to a serving plate and serve.

BLACK PEPPER BEEF

Here's a popular dish you'll enjoy. For a variation, use a few tablespoons of prepared black pepper sauce in place of the hoisin sauce, soy sauce, and black pepper. Serve over Panfried Noodles (page 199) with a side dish of Braised Mushrooms (page 187).

MAKES 4 SERVINGS

Marinade

1 tablespoon regular soy sauce or dark soy sauce

2 teaspoons cornstarch

1 teaspoon black pepper

2 cloves garlic, minced

1 teaspoon minced ginger

¾ pound flank steak, thinly sliced across the grain

Sauce

¼ cup chicken broth

2 tablespoons hoisin sauce

2 teaspoons soy sauce

2 teaspoons sesame oil

1 tablespoon vegetable oil

2 small dried red chilies

½ yellow onion, cut into ½-inch cubes

1 carrot, peeled and thinly sliced on the diagonal

To make the marinade, combine all the ingredients in a bowl and mix well. Add the beef and stir to coat evenly. Let stand for 10 minutes.

To make the sauce, combine all the ingredients in a small bowl and mix well.

Place a stir-fry pan over high heat until hot. Add the oil, swirling to coat the sides. Add the chilies and cook, stirring, until very lightly browned, about 45 seconds. Add the beef, onion, and carrot and stir-fry until the onion begins to brown on the edges, about 2 minutes. Add the sauce and cook, stirring, until the carrot is tender-crisp and the meat is cooked, 2 to 3 minutes.

Transfer to a serving plate and serve.

BEEF AND TOFU STIR-FRY

Another take on the popular Sichuan dish *ma pa tofu*. If you have some ground beef on hand, you can substitute it for the flank steak. I typically serve a mild soup, vegetables, and a rice dish for a complete meal.

Marinade

- 1 tablespoon soy sauce
- 1 tablespoon Chinese rice wine or dry sherry
- 2 teaspoons cornstarch

¾ **pound flank steak,** cut into ½-inch cubes

Sauce

- ⅓ cup chicken broth
- 1 tablespoon oyster-flavored sauce
- 1 teaspoon chili garlic sauce

- 1 tablespoon vegetable oil
- 2 teaspoons minced ginger
- ½ **yellow onion,** chopped

One **14-ounce package firm tofu,** drained and cut into ½-inch cubes

- 1 **teaspoon cornstarch,** dissolved in 2 teaspoons water

MAKES 4 SERVINGS

To make the marinade, combine all the ingredients in a bowl and mix well. Add the beef and stir to coat evenly. Let stand for 10 minutes.

To make the sauce, combine all the ingredients in a small bowl and mix well.

Place a stir-fry pan over high heat until hot. Add the oil, swirling to coat the sides. Add the ginger and onion and cook, stirring, until fragrant, about 1 minute. Add the beef and stir-fry until it is no longer pink in the center, about 2 minutes. Add the tofu and sauce and bring to a boil, stirring constantly. Add the cornstarch solution and cook, stirring, until the sauce boils and thickens, about 20 seconds.

Transfer to a serving plate and serve.

CRUNCHY APPLE BEEF

While in Taiwan, I tried a dish at the Ye Yeun restaurant in Taipei that inspired me to create this savory stir-fry using crisp, tart Granny Smith apples. Leave the peel on the apple for texture and visual appeal. Chef Chan, who oversees the kitchen at Ye Yeun, participates in a design and recipe competition every year. I wonder what he will come up with next!

Marinade

- 2 teaspoons soy sauce
- 1 teaspoon cornstarch

- ¾ **pound flank steak,** cut into ½-inch cubes
  Grated zest of ½ lemon
- 1 **tablespoon fresh lemon juice**
- ¼ **teaspoon Chinese five-spice powder**
- 1 **Granny Smith apple,** cored and cut into ½-inch cubes
- 1 **tablespoon vegetable oil**
- ½ **red bell pepper,** seeded and cut into ½-inch dice
- ½ **green bell pepper,** seeded and cut into ½-inch dice
- 3 **green onions,** cut into 2-inch lengths

To make the marinade, combine the soy sauce and cornstarch in a bowl and mix well. Add the beef and stir to coat evenly. Let stand for 10 minutes.

In a small bowl, combine the lemon zest, lemon juice, and five-spice powder and mix well. Add the apple and stir to coat evenly.

Place a stir-fry pan over high heat until hot. Add the oil, swirling to coat the sides. Add the beef and cook, stirring, until rare, about 2 minutes. Add the apple mixture, bell peppers, and green onions and cook, stirring, until the apples are tender-crisp, about 2 minutes.

Transfer to a serving plate and serve.

LEMON-PEPPER BEEF

A trip to Vietnam influenced this new favorite dish of mine. This is not your usual lemon sauce: it is light and almost glazes the tender morsels of meat. Be sure to use a piece of beef that is lightly marbled with fat.

MAKES 3 SERVINGS

Marinade

- 1 teaspoon cornstarch
- 2 teaspoons fish sauce

- ¾ **pound beef tri-tip,** cut into 1-inch cubes

Sauce

- 2 tablespoons fresh lemon juice
- 1 tablespoon black pepper
- 2 teaspoons sugar

- 1 tablespoon vegetable oil
- 1 teaspoon butter
- 2 cloves garlic, thinly sliced
- 1 lemongrass stalk, bottom 4 inches only, minced
- 2 walnut-sized shallots, thinly sliced

To make the marinade, combine the cornstarch and fish sauce in a bowl and mix well. Add the beef and stir to coat evenly. Let stand for 10 minutes.

To make the sauce, combine all the ingredients in a small bowl and stir until the sugar is dissolved.

Place a stir-fry pan over high heat until hot. Add the oil and butter and stir until the butter melts. Add the garlic and lemongrass and cook, stirring, until fragrant, about 30 seconds. Add the beef and stir-fry until it is seared on the outside and slightly pink in the center, about 4 minutes. Add shallots and cook until translucent. Add the sauce and toss to coat the meat evenly.

Transfer to a serving plate and serve.

BOLD BASIL BEEF

If you can find Thai basil, which has a more complex flavor than traditional basil, use it for this dish. Add the basil at the very end to retain some of its bright green color. Serve the beef with Pineapple Hot-and-Sour Soup (page 75), Tropical Beef (page 147), and steamed rice.

Marinade

- 1 **tablespoon dark soy sauce**
- 1 **tablespoon cornstarch**

- 1 **pound flank steak,** thinly sliced across the grain
- 1 **tablespoon vegetable oil**
- 1 **walnut-sized shallot,** thinly sliced into rings
- 1 **jalapeño chili,** thinly sliced into rings
- ½ **cup lightly packed Thai basil or regular basil leaves**

MAKES 4 SERVINGS

To make the marinade, combine the soy sauce and cornstarch in a bowl and mix well. Add the beef and stir to coat evenly. Let stand for 10 minutes.

Place a stir-fry pan over high heat until hot. Add the oil, swirling to coat the sides. Add the shallot and chili and cook, stirring, until fragrant, about 20 seconds. Add the beef and stir-fry until barely pink in the center, 3 to 4 minutes.

Remove from the heat and stir in the basil leaves. Transfer to a serving plate and serve.

SESAME-ORANGE BEEF

My recent travels have renewed my interest in using fruit in savory dishes. The orange has many meanings in Chinese culture, but primarily it is a symbol of prosperity and wealth. Something we can all enjoy!

Marinade

2 teaspoons cornstarch

2 teaspoons soy sauce

¾ **pound beef tri-tip,** thinly sliced across the grain

Sauce

¼ cup fresh orange juice

2 tablespoons oyster-flavored sauce

1 tablespoon honey

2 teaspoons cornstarch

1 tablespoon sesame seeds

2 tablespoons vegetable oil

1 teaspoon minced ginger

2 oranges, segmented (page 16)

½ cup pineapple chunks

To make the marinade, combine the cornstarch and soy sauce in a bowl and mix well. Add the beef and stir to coat evenly. Let stand for 10 minutes.

To make the sauce, combine all the ingredients in a small bowl and stir until the honey dissolves. Set aside.

In a small frying pan, toast the sesame seeds over medium heat, shaking the pan frequently, until lightly colored, 3 to 4 minutes. Immediately pour onto a plate to cool.

Place a stir-fry pan over high heat until hot. Add the oil, swirling to coat the sides. Add the ginger and cook, stirring, until fragrant, about 10 seconds. Add the beef and stir-fry until caramelized on the edges and still slightly pink in the center, 2 to 3 minutes. Add the sauce and cook, stirring, until the sauce boils and thickens slightly, about 20 seconds. Stir in the orange segments and pineapple chunks and cook for 30 seconds to heat through.

Transfer to a serving plate, sprinkle with the sesame seeds, and serve.

MEAT SAUCE OVER RICE STICK NOODLES

Serving a rich, meaty sauce over noodles is popular in noodle shops all over Asia. I love the versatility of this dish, which can instead be served over wheat noodles or steamed rice. You can also add some rich broth and pickled vegetables to the basic sauce. Both versions are delicious. It is important to use dark soy sauce in this dish. It adds an intensity that you cannot get with regular soy sauce.

MAKES 4 SERVINGS

Marinade

- 2 teaspoons dark soy sauce
- 2 teaspoons Chinese rice wine or dry sherry
- 1 tablespoon cornstarch

- ¾ pound ground pork, beef, or chicken

Sauce

- ¾ cup chicken broth
- 2 tablespoons oyster-flavored sauce
- 1 tablespoon hoisin sauce
- 1 tablespoon sesame oil
- 2 teaspoons dark soy sauce
- 2 teaspoons chili garlic sauce
- ⅛ teaspoon white pepper

- 1 tablespoon vegetable oil
- 2 tablespoons minced garlic
- 2 green onions, chopped
- 2 teaspoons cornstarch dissolved in 1 tablespoon water
- 4 cups cooked rice stick noodles
  Chopped fresh cilantro and green onions for garnish

To make the marinade, combine all the ingredients in a bowl and mix well. Add the ground meat and stir to distribute evenly. Let stand for 10 minutes.

To make the sauce, combine all the ingredients in a bowl and mix well.

Place a stir-fry pan over high heat until hot. Add the oil, swirling to coat the sides. Add the garlic and the 2 green onions and cook, stirring, until fragrant, about 20 seconds. Add the ground meat and stir-fry until browned and crumbly, about 3 minutes. Add the sauce and bring to a boil. Add the cornstarch solution and cook, stirring, until the sauce boils and thickens, about 30 seconds. Divide the cooked noodles among 4 large soup bowls. Ladle about ¾ cup of the meat sauce over the noodles in each bowl. Garnish with the cilantro and green onions and serve.

DYNASTY BURGER

Even the most all-American dishes can be made with Asian flavors. The hamburger is a traditional centerpiece of a backyard barbecue, and when my family barbecues, I give the meal an Asian twist. To round out the menu, I quickly pickle cucumbers, toss together coleslaw, and open a bag of taro or sweet potato chips.

Meat Patties

- 1 pound ground beef
- 2 tablespoons soy sauce
- 1 tablespoon hoisin sauce
- 1 tablespoon chopped fresh cilantro
- 2 teaspoons sesame oil
- 1 teaspoon grated ginger

Sauce

- ¼ cup purchased barbecue sauce
- ¼ cup hoisin sauce
- 2 teaspoons chili garlic sauce
- 2 teaspoons sesame oil

- 4 hamburger buns
- 4 lettuce leaves
- 1 **tomato,** thinly sliced
- 1 **small red onion,** thinly sliced

To make the meat patties, combine all the ingredients in a bowl and mix well. Divide the mixture into 4 equal portions. Lightly shape each portion into a patty about 4 inches in diameter. Set aside.

To make the sauce, combine all the ingredients in a small bowl and mix well.

Place a grill pan over high heat until hot. Place the patties on the pan and cook, turning once, until done to your liking, 3 to 4 minutes on each side for medium-rare. Remove the pan from the heat and top each burger with 1 tablespoon of the sauce.

Serve the patties in the hamburger buns with the lettuce, tomato, and onion.

GRILLED BEEF VIETNAMESE STREET SANDWICH

You can use other types of meat, such as pork or chicken, or even pressed tofu, for these delicious sandwiches, which are good for lunch. The meat can be served with a variety of other dishes if you choose not to make sandwiches: Wo Ti's Garlicky Romaine Salad (page 64), Simple Sesame Noodles (page 204), or Garlicky Peanut Noodles (page 208).

MAKES 4 SERVINGS

Marinade

2 tablespoons fish sauce

1 tablespoon soy sauce

2 teaspoons sugar

1 lemongrass stalk, bottom 4 inches only, minced

2 cloves garlic, minced

1 tablespoon chopped fresh mint

1 teaspoon chili garlic sauce

¾ pound beef tri-tip or flank steak, thinly sliced across the grain on the diagonal

Seasoned Mayonnaise

½ cup mayonnaise

1 tablespoon oyster-flavored sauce

1 teaspoon sesame oil

1 teaspoon vegetable oil

4 soft French rolls, split and lightly toasted

¾ cup fresh cilantro stems and leaves

1 cup Sweet-and-Sour Shredded Carrots (page 37)

1 jalapeño chili, thinly sliced

To make the marinade, combine all the ingredients in a bowl and mix well. Add the beef and stir to coat evenly. Let stand for 10 minutes.

To make the seasoned mayonnaise, combine all the ingredients in a small bowl and mix well. Set aside.

Place a grill pan over medium-high heat until hot. Brush with the vegetable oil. Place the beef strips on the pan and cook, turning once, until no longer pink, about 2 minutes on each side. Remove from the heat.

Spread the seasoned mayonnaise on the cut sides of each roll. Divide the beef, cilantro, carrots, and chili evenly among the rolls, placing them on one side of each roll. Close the rolls and serve.

CHILI-BRAISED BEEF NOODLE BOWL

This is one of the few recipes that I have included that is not both quick and easy. It's easy, but it is not that quick. Braised dishes are tailored for weekend cooking. Here, it takes 15 minutes to start the meat. Then, while it simmers, you can turn to other things in the house. The noodle bowl doesn't need to be served the same day; let it cool and refrigerate it, then eat it on a busy weeknight. Reheat it in the broth while you cook the noodles and bok choy.

MAKES 6 TO 8 SERVINGS

1 tablespoon vegetable oil

2 pounds beef brisket or well-marbled boneless pot roast

Braising Liquid

6 cups chicken broth

½ cup soy sauce

1 tablespoon Chinese rice wine or dry sherry

1 tablespoon chili bean sauce or chili garlic sauce

10 cloves garlic, peeled and lightly crushed

3 quarter-sized slices ginger, lightly crushed

2 green onions, cut into 2-inch lengths

3 whole star anise

1 teaspoon sugar

½ teaspoon black pepper

½ teaspoon Chinese five-spice powder

16 ounces fresh Chinese egg noodles

6 baby bok choy, cut lengthwise into quarters

2 tablespoons chopped Sichuan preserved vegetable (optional)

2 green onions, chopped

Place a Dutch oven over medium-high heat until hot. Add the oil, swirling to coat the bottom. Place the meat in the pan and brown for 2 minutes on each side. Add all the braising liquid ingredients and bring to a boil. Reduce the heat to low, cover, and simmer until the beef is tender when pierced, 2 to 2 ½ hours.

Near serving time, bring a large pot filled with water to a boil over high heat. Add the noodles and cook according to package directions. Drain, rinse with cold water, and drain again. Divide the noodles among 6 to 8 large soup bowls.

Meanwhile, bring a saucepan filled with water to a boil, add the bok choy, and cook until tender, 2 to 3 minutes. Drain and place over the noodles in each bowl.

Remove the meat from the braising liquid and cut into small chunks. Place in the bowls with the noodles. Ladle the hot broth over the noodles. Garnish with the preserved vegetable (if desired) and green onions and serve.

BLACK TEA–BRAISED SHORT RIBS

These delectable little ribs take about 1½ hours to cook, but are well worth the time. I leave them cooking on the stove and spend some time in my garden or with my pet koi. Warning: Purchase the ribs carefully. If you buy the thinly sliced ribs across the bone, sometimes called country-style ribs, you will need to cook them only about half the time indicated in the recipe. Serve with a bowl of steamed rice.

Marinade

- ¼ cup dark soy sauce
- 2 tablespoons regular soy sauce
- 2 teaspoons cornstarch

- 2 pounds beef short ribs
- 1 tablespoon vegetable oil
- 4 quarter-sized slices ginger, lightly crushed
- 2 green onions, cut into 2-inch lengths
- 4 cups chicken broth
- 6 bags black tea
- ¼ cup Chinese rice wine or dry sherry
- ⅓ cup packed brown sugar
- 1 whole star anise
- 2 cinnamon sticks
- 1 pound daikon, peeled and cut into 1-inch cubes
- 2 carrots, peeled and roll-cut (see page 16)

To make the marinade, combine all the ingredients in a large bowl and mix well. Add the short ribs and stir to coat evenly. Let stand for 10 minutes.

Place a large saucepan over high heat until hot. Add the oil, swirling to coat the bottom. Add the ginger and green onions and cook, stirring, until fragrant, about 10 seconds. Reduce the heat to medium and add the broth, tea bags, wine, brown sugar, star anise, cinnamon sticks, and beef. Bring to a boil, reduce the heat to low, cover, and simmer until the meat is tender, about 1 hour. Add the daikon and carrots, cover, and simmer until the vegetables are tender, about 20 minutes.

Transfer to a shallow serving bowl and serve.

KOREAN-STYLE LAMB CHOPS

Plan on 2 or 3 lamb chops per person. You'll find both whole racks of lamb, with about 8 ribs per rack, and precut chops in the meat sections of most supermarkets. Since this recipe is designed for quick cooking, you will need to cut the chops apart if you buy a rack. Serve this fiery dish with Rustic Smashed Potatoes (page 188) and Flash-Fried Asparagus and Long Beans (page 175). If you can find Korean chili paste, use it in place of the chili garlic sauce.

MAKES 4 SERVINGS

Marinade

⅓ cup soy sauce

1 tablespoon sesame oil

1 teaspoon rice vinegar

1½ tablespoons sugar

2 teaspoons chili garlic sauce or Korean chili paste

2 teaspoons sesame paste or tahini

3 cloves garlic, minced

1 rack of lamb, cut into chops (at least 8 chops total)

1 teaspoon vegetable oil

To make the marinade, combine all the ingredients in a large bowl and mix well. Add the lamb and turn to coat evenly. Let stand at room temperature for 10 minutes, or cover and refrigerate for up to 4 hours.

Place a grill pan over medium-high heat until hot. Brush with the oil. Remove the lamb chops from the marinade and pour the marinade into a small saucepan. Place the chops on the grill pan and cook, turning once, until medium-rare, about 6 minutes on each side. While the lamb is cooking, place the marinade over medium-high heat and bring to a boil. Cook, stirring, for 1 minute. Remove from the heat.

Transfer the lamb chops to a serving plate, pour the hot marinade over the top, and serve.

SICHUAN GARLIC LAMB

If you don't have dark soy sauce, have no fear! Use regular soy sauce in its place. The dish will not be as rich, but it will still be as delicious!

MAKES 4 SERVINGS

Marinade

- 2 **teaspoons dark soy sauce**
- 2 **teaspoons cornstarch**
- ¼ **teaspoon Chinese five-spice powder**

- 1 **pound tender boneless lamb from the leg or loin,** thinly sliced across the grain
- 1 **tablespoon vegetable oil**
- 3 **cloves garlic,** minced
- 1 **jalapeño chili,** seeded and chopped
- 2 **tablespoons hoisin sauce**
- 1 **tablespoon chili garlic sauce**
- 2 **tablespoons coarsely chopped fresh mint**

To make the marinade, combine all the ingredients in a bowl and mix well. Add the lamb and stir to coat evenly. Let stand for 10 minutes.

Place a stir-fry pan over high heat until hot. Add the oil, swirling to coat the sides. Add the garlic and chili and cook, stirring, until fragrant, about 15 seconds. Add the lamb and stir-fry until barely pink, 2 to 3 minutes. Add the hoisin sauce and chili garlic sauce and cook for 30 seconds.

Remove from the heat and stir in the mint. Transfer to a serving plate and serve.

WOK-TOSSED PORK WITH MISO GLAZE

Here's another way to use miso. Pork is a nice lean option, but the recipe can also be made with chicken or turkey. Have a menu of three different soy products, the whole bean, miso, and tofu, by serving Soybean Fried Rice (page 190) and Miso Soup (page 72) with the pork.

MAKES 4 SERVINGS

1 **pound boneless pork,** thinly sliced

1 **teaspoon soy sauce**

1 **teaspoon cornstarch**

Sauce

½ **cup chicken broth**

1½ **tablespoons white miso**

1 **tablespoon Chinese rice wine or dry sherry**

1 **tablespoon sweet chili sauce**

1 **tablespoon vegetable oil**

½ **yellow onion,** cut into ½-inch cubes

In a bowl, combine the pork, soy sauce, and cornstarch and mix well.

To make the sauce, combine all the ingredients in a small bowl and mix well.

Place a stir-fry pan over high heat until hot. Add the oil, swirling to coat the sides. Add the onion and cook, stirring, until fragrant, about 20 seconds. Add the pork and stir-fry until it is no longer pink, 2½ to 3 minutes. Add the sauce, bring to a boil, and cook until the sauce thickens slightly, about 30 seconds. Transfer to a serving plate and serve.

TAIWANESE PORK CHOPS

This dish is part of a typical workingman's lunch in Taiwan, which also includes a bowl of broth (page 34), some cooked egg noodles, Marbled Tea Eggs (page 43), and Tangy Bean Sprout Salad (page 58). Quick, filling, and delicious! Try the same marinade with chicken breasts. These tasty chops can also be served with Simple Sesame Noodles (page 204) or just with the dipping sauce.

MAKES 4 SERVINGS

Marinade

- 1 **egg,** lightly beaten
- 2 **tablespoons soy sauce**
- 1 **tablespoon Chinese rice wine or dry sherry**
- 1 **tablespoon ketchup**
- 1 **tablespoon oyster-flavored sauce**
- 1½ **teaspoons sesame oil**
- 1 **tablespoon cornstarch**
- ¼ **teaspoon white pepper**

- 8 **boneless pork chops (each about ½ inch thick)**

Dipping Sauce

- 2 **tablespoons ketchup**
- 2 **tablespoons oyster-flavored sauce**
- 2 **teaspoons sesame oil**

Vegetable oil for shallow-frying
All-purpose flour for dusting

To make the marinade, combine all the ingredients in a large bowl and mix well. Add the pork chops and stir to coat evenly. Let stand at room temperature for 20 minutes, or cover and refrigerate for up to 4 hours. To make the dipping sauce, combine all the ingredients in a small bowl and mix well. Set aside.

Pour oil to a depth of 1 inch into a 2-quart saucepan and heat to 350°F on a deep-frying thermometer. Working in batches, remove the pork chops from the marinade, drain briefly, and dust evenly with flour, shaking off the excess. Slide the chops into the hot oil and fry, turning once, until golden brown and cooked through, about 2 minutes on each side. Remove with a slotted spoon and drain on paper towels. Keep warm while you cook the remaining chops.

Arrange the pork chops on a serving plate and serve with the dipping sauce.

GLAZED GRILLED PORK CHOPS

Both *char siu* sauce and hoisin sauce have a high sugar content, so watch carefully when using them in this recipe to avoid burning the chops. Reduce the heat under the grill pan if the chops begin to scorch.

MAKES 4 SERVINGS

Marinade

½   cup *char siu* sauce or hoisin sauce

2   tablespoons sesame oil

2   tablespoons Chinese rice wine or dry sherry

1   clove garlic, minced

1   walnut-sized shallot, minced

4   boneless loin pork chops (each about 1 inch thick)

1   teaspoon vegetable oil

⅓   cup chicken broth

To make the marinade, combine all the ingredients in a bowl and mix well. Add the pork chops and turn to coat evenly. Let stand at room temperature for 10 minutes, or cover and refrigerate for up to 4 hours, turning the pork occasionally in the marinade.

Place a grill pan over medium-high heat until hot. Brush with the oil. Place the pork chops on the pan, reserving the marinade. Cook, turning occasionally and basting with the marinade, until the meat is no longer pink in the center, about 5 minutes on each side.

In a small saucepan, combine the remaining marinade and broth and bring to a boil over high heat. Reduce the heat to medium-low and simmer until the sauce thickens slightly, about 3 minutes.

Transfer the pork chops to a serving plate, brush the sauce on the chops, and serve.

QUICK CHAR SIU

Traditional Chinese barbecued pork, known as *char siu* in Cantonese, is marinated overnight and roasted slowly in the oven. Here, the pork is cut into thin strips, marinated for a mere 10 minutes, and quickly broiled for a similar flavor. Add the pork to a stir-fry, or use as a garnish for Monday-Night Dumpling Soup (page 98) or Great Wall Hoisin Pizza (page 126).

Marinade

- ⅓ cup hoisin sauce or *char siu* sauce
- ¼ cup Chinese rice wine or dry sherry
- 3 tablespoons honey
- 2 tablespoons sesame oil
- 1 clove garlic, finely minced
- 1 tablespoon grated ginger
- ½ teaspoon Chinese five-spice powder

- 1 pound boneless pork butt or other well-marbled pork cut

To make the marinade, combine all the ingredients in a bowl and mix well. Cut the meat into strips ½ inch thick and about 2 inches wide. Place in the marinade and turn to coat evenly. Let stand for 10 minutes at room temperature, or, for a richer flavor, cover and refrigerate overnight.

Preheat the broiler.

Place a rack in an aluminum foil-lined baking pan. Arrange the meat strips in a single layer on the rack, reserving the marinade. Slip under the broiler 3 to 4 inches from the heat and broil, turning once and basting twice with the marinade, until the pork is no longer pink in the center, about 7 minutes on each side.

Pour the remaining marinade in a small saucepan and bring to a boil over high heat. Remove from the heat.

Transfer the pork to a plate and brush the heated marinade over the top. Let stand for 10 minutes before slicing.

VEGETABLES, RICE & NOODLES

THREE-MINUTE BABY BOK CHOY

With a strong flame and quick hands, it takes only about three minutes to cook this delicious side dish. The Cantonese-inspired sauce is great on a variety of vegetables. Try using asparagus, *gai lan*, or summer squash instead of the bok choy. Like most Chinese chefs, I'll trim off the top 1 inch from the leaves of the bok choy. But this is primarily for looks, and home cooks do not need to do it.

MAKES 4 SERVINGS

Sauce

- ⅓ cup chicken broth
- 2 tablespoons Chinese rice wine or dry sherry
- ½ teaspoon sesame oil
- 1 teaspoon cornstarch
- 1 teaspoon black bean garlic sauce
- ¼ teaspoon white pepper

- 1 tablespoon vegetable oil
- 1 or 2 cloves garlic, minced
- 1 pound baby bok choy, cut lengthwise into quarters

To make the sauce, combine all the ingredients in a small bowl and stir to dissolve the cornstarch.

Place a stir-fry pan over high heat until hot. Add the oil, swirling to coat the sides. Add the garlic and cook, stirring, until fragrant, about 10 seconds. Add the bok choy and stir-fry until tender-crisp, 1½ to 2 minutes. Add the sauce and cook, stirring, until the sauce thickens slightly and lightly coats the bok choy, about 30 seconds.

Transfer to a serving plate and serve.

TOASTED SESAME GREENS

Leafy green vegetables are a favorite at my family dinner table. Use any leafy green of your choice. Check out the variety of Asian greens, such as water spinach or Chinese mustard, at Asian markets. Many Asian greens are beginning to find their way into supermarkets as well. Adjust the cooking time so that the green you use is cooked to desired tenderness, as some leaves are a bit tougher and have stems that require more time.

MAKES 3 SERVINGS

1 tablespoon sesame seeds

2 teaspoons vegetable oil

2 teaspoons chopped ginger

3/4 pound spinach or other leafy green

1/4 cup vegetable broth

1 teaspoon sesame oil

1 teaspoon soy sauce

In a small frying pan, toast the sesame seeds over medium heat, shaking the pan frequently, until lightly colored, 3 to 4 minutes. Immediately pour onto a plate to cool. Place a large saucepan over high heat until hot. Add the oil, swirling to coat the bottom. Add the ginger and cook, stirring, until fragrant, about 10 seconds. Add the spinach and broth and stir once, then cover. Reduce the heat to medium and cook, stirring once, until the greens are wilted, about 2 minutes. Add the sesame oil, soy sauce, and sesame seeds and toss to distribute the seasonings. Transfer to a serving plate and serve.

FLASH-FRIED ASPARAGUS AND LONG BEANS

Here is a spicy way to fix asparagus, my favorite California vegetable. For a complete meal, serve with another stir-fry or Tea-Smoked Salmon (page 124) and with a bowl of steamed rice.

MAKES 4 SERVINGS

1 **pound asparagus**

½ **pound Chinese long beans**

2 **teaspoons vegetable oil**

2 **cloves garlic,** minced

2 **green onions,** chopped

⅓ **cup chicken broth**

2 **teaspoons soy sauce**

1 **teaspoon sugar**

½ **teaspoon red chili flakes**

½ **teaspoon cornstarch,** dissolved in
   2 teaspoons water

Trim off the tough ends from the asparagus. Cut the spears on the diagonal into 2-inch pieces. Place the asparagus tips in a separate pile. Trim the long beans and cut on the diagonal into 2-inch pieces.

Place a stir-fry pan over high heat until hot. Add the oil, swirling to coat the sides. Add the garlic and green onions and cook, stirring, until fragrant, about 20 seconds. Add the long beans and stir-fry until almost tender, about 2 minutes. Add a few drops of water if the pan appears dry. Add the asparagus stems and stir-fry for 2 more minutes. Add the asparagus tips, broth, soy sauce, sugar, and red chili flakes and stir well. Cover and cook until the asparagus is tender-crisp, 1 to 2 minutes. Add the cornstarch solution and cook, stirring, until the sauce boils and thickens, about 30 seconds.

Transfer to a serving plate and serve.

GRILLED MISO-GLAZED EGGPLANT

Asian eggplant has a mild and sweet flavor and a tender skin that does not need to be peeled. For a fancy presentation, cut the eggplant like a fan, and serve one fan to each of your guests.

MAKES 4 SERVINGS

1 teaspoon vegetable oil

4 **Asian eggplants,** cut lengthwise into slices
⅓ inch thick

Sauce

¼ cup purchased teriyaki sauce

3 tablespoons vegetable broth

2 tablespoons white miso

¼ teaspoon red chili flakes

Heat a grill pan over medium-high heat until hot. Brush the pan with the oil. Place the eggplant slices on the pan and cook, turning once, until tender, about 2 minutes total.

To make the sauce, combine all the ingredients in a small saucepan and whisk to blend evenly. Bring to a boil over medium-high heat, reduce the heat to low, and simmer for 2 minutes.

To serve, arrange the eggplants, in an overlapping pattern, on a serving plate and drizzle with the sauce.

ALMOND BABY BOK CHOY

I was snacking on almonds in the kitchen and thought they'd be a good touch to a simple dish. Their mild flavor allows the sweetness of the baby bok choy to shine through. As already noted, most Chinese chefs trim off the top inch of the bok choy leaves for a better appearance. If you choose, you can deep-fry the trimmed tops. Shred them, deep-fry until crisp, and use as a garnish.

½ cup slivered blanched almonds

¼ cup chicken or vegetable broth

¼ teaspoon sugar

⅛ teaspoon white pepper

1 tablespoon vegetable oil

1 teaspoon minced ginger

1 pound baby bok choy, cut lengthwise into quarters

MAKES 4 SERVINGS

In a small frying pan, toast the nuts over medium heat, shaking the pan frequently, until lightly browned, 3 to 4 minutes. Immediately pour onto a plate to cool.

In a small bowl, combine the broth, sugar, and pepper and stir until the sugar dissolves. Place a stir-fry pan over high heat until hot. Add the oil, swirling to coat the sides. Add the ginger and cook, stirring, until fragrant, about 10 seconds. Add the bok choy and stir-fry until tender-crisp, 2 to 3 minutes. Add the broth mixture and toss until the bok choy is evenly coated.

Transfer to a serving plate, sprinkle with the almonds, and serve.

GINGER SUGAR SNAP PEAS

This dish is a snap to make. I have included the step of parboiling the peas and corn, as it makes a superior dish, but you can skip it and stir-fry the vegetables longer. Remember, though, parboiling removes any of the tinny flavor that the corn picks up from being canned.

MAKES 4 SERVINGS

1 **pound sugar snap peas**

10 **ears baby corn,** cut in half on the diagonal

Sauce

¼ **cup Chinese rice wine or dry sherry**

1 **tablespoon oyster-flavored sauce**

1½ **teaspoons chili garlic sauce**

1 **teaspoon sugar**

¼ **teaspoon salt**

1 **tablespoon vegetable oil**

3 **cloves garlic,** minced

1 **tablespoon minced ginger**

Bring a large pot filled with water to a boil over high heat. Add the sugar snap peas and baby corn and cook until the sugar snap peas are bright green and tender-crisp, about 1½ minutes. Drain, rinse with cold water, and drain again. Set aside.

To make the sauce, combine all the ingredients in a small bowl and stir until the sugar dissolves. Set aside.

Place a stir-fry pan over high heat until hot. Add the oil, swirling to coat the sides. Add the garlic and ginger and cook, stirring, until fragrant, about 15 seconds. Add the sugar snap peas, baby corn, and sauce and stir-fry for 1 minute to heat through.

Transfer to a serving plate and serve.

BROCCOLI AND CAULIFLOWER STIR-FRY

Simple, healthful, and versatile describe this colorful dish. To transform it into a main dish, add ½ pound cubed firm tofu or chicken. To save time cutting broccoli and cauliflower florets, purchase them precut and prewashed in bags. A ³⁄₄-pound bag is the perfect amount for the recipe.

2 teaspoons vegetable oil

2 cloves garlic, minced

2 cups bite-sized broccoli florets

1 cup bite-sized cauliflower florets

³⁄₄ cup chicken or vegetable broth

2 tablespoons oyster-flavored sauce

Place a stir-fry pan over high heat until hot. Add the oil, swirling to coat the sides. Add the garlic and cook, stirring, until fragrant, about 10 seconds. Add the broccoli and cauliflower and stir-fry for 2 minutes. Add the broth, cover, reduce the heat to medium, and cook until tender, 3 to 4 minutes. Add the oyster-flavored sauce and toss to coat evenly. Transfer to a serving plate and serve.

EGGPLANT IN PLUM SAUCE

Oil-blanching is common in Chinese cuisine. It is especially important in this dish for two reasons: First, the hot oil seals the outside of the eggplant so it won't absorb additional oil. Second, it helps the eggplant retain its beautiful bright purple color.

MAKES 4 SERVINGS

Sauce

- 3 tablespoons plum sauce
- 2 tablespoons plum wine or Chinese rice wine
- 2 teaspoons sesame oil
- 1 teaspoon regular soy sauce
- 1 teaspoon dark soy sauce

- Vegetable oil for deep-frying
- 1 pound Asian eggplants, roll-cut (see page 16)
- 3 cloves garlic, chopped

To make the sauce, combine all the ingredients in a small bowl and whisk to blend evenly. Set aside.

Pour oil to a depth of 2 inches into a 3-quart saucepan and heat to 350°F on a deep-frying thermometer. Working in batches, add the eggplant pieces and cook, turning occasionally, until golden brown, about 3 minutes. Remove with a slotted spoon and drain on paper towels.

Heat a stir-fry pan over high heat until hot. Add 2 teaspoons of the frying oil and swirl to coat the sides. Add the garlic and cook, stirring, until fragrant, about 20 seconds. Add the eggplant and the sauce and bring to a boil. Cook, stirring, for 1 minute.

Transfer to a serving plate and serve.

SIMPLY GAI LAN

Eat more greens! *Gai lan*, or Chinese broccoli, is a great accompaniment to almost any dinner. When I cook dense vegetables such as this one in boiling water, I add a little bit of oil to the water to give the vegetable a nice sheen.

MAKES 4 SERVINGS

1 pound Chinese broccoli or regular broccoli

Blanching Water
2 quarts (8 cups) water
2 teaspoons vegetable oil
1 teaspoon salt

2 teaspoons vegetable oil
2 teaspoons minced ginger
2 tablespoons Chinese rice wine or dry sherry
1 teaspoon soy sauce
¼ teaspoon salt

If using Chinese broccoli, trim the ends of the stems but leave whole. If using regular broccoli, remove the broccoli florets from the stems. Cut the florets into bite-sized pieces, and peel the stems and cut into slices on the diagonal.

To prepare the blanching water, combine all the ingredients in a large saucepan and bring to a boil. Add the broccoli and cook until tender-crisp, about 4 minutes. Drain, rinse with cold water, and drain again.

Place a stir-fry pan over high heat until hot. Add the oil, swirling to coat the sides. Add the ginger and cook, stirring, until fragrant, about 10 seconds. Add the broccoli, wine, soy sauce, and salt and stir-fry until the liquid has reduced by half, about 1 minute.

Transfer to a serving plate and serve.

SWISS CHARD WITH BLACK BEAN GARLIC SAUCE

This dish brings back memories from my childhood. We ate Swiss chard all the time, since the vegetable grew rapidly and didn't take much garden space. As a time-saver, look for bagged Swiss chard already cut and cleaned.

1 pound Swiss chard

Seasoning Mixture
1 tablespoon black bean garlic sauce
1 tablespoon oyster-flavored sauce
1½ teaspoons sugar

2 teaspoons vegetable oil
2 cloves garlic, minced
¼ cup sliced water chestnuts
¼ cup chicken broth

Cut the Swiss chard stems from the leaves. Thinly slice the stems and coarsely chop the leaves. Set aside.

To make the seasoning mixture, combine all the ingredients in a small bowl and mix well. Place a stir-fry pan over high heat until hot. Add the oil, swirling to coat the sides. Add the garlic and cook, stirring, until fragrant, about 10 seconds. Add the seasoning mixture, chard, and water chestnuts and stir well. Add the broth, reduce the heat to medium, cover, and cook until the chard is tender, about 5 minutes.

Stir well, transfer to a serving plate, and serve.

BUDDHIST BRAISED WINTER SQUASH

Here's a delicious side dish that is hearty enough to be served as the main course for a vegetarian dinner. The combination of creamy *kabocha* squash and coconut milk makes this dish special. If you find it difficult to cut the *kabocha* squash, pop it in the microwave oven for 2 minutes to soften slightly before cutting.

MAKES 4 TO 6 SERVINGS

5 dried wood ears (optional)

2 cups sliced, peeled *kabocha* or other firm winter squash

2 cups sliced, peeled sweet potatoes

2 cups unsweetened coconut milk

1 cup vegetable broth

1 small zucchini, thinly sliced

1 tablespoon soy sauce

⅓ cup fresh cilantro leaves

½ cup pistachio nuts

In a bowl, soak the wood ears in warm water to cover until softened, about 10 minutes; drain. Cut into narrow strips.

In a large saucepan, combine the squash, sweet potatoes, wood ears, coconut milk, and broth. Bring to a boil over medium-high heat, reduce the heat to low, and simmer until the sweet potatoes are tender, about 15 minutes. Add the zucchini and soy sauce, increase the heat to medium-high, and bring to a boil. Cook until the zucchini is tender, about 2 minutes.

Transfer to a shallow bowl, garnish with the cilantro and nuts, and serve.

GINGERY BUTTERNUT SQUASH

Butternut squash can be a difficult vegetable to cut, so arm yourself with a heavy knife. Or make it easy on yourself and purchase a bag of peeled and cut butternut squash.

2   teaspoons vegetable oil

2   tablespoons chopped ginger

1½   cups cubed, peeled butternut squash

¾   cup chicken broth

1   zucchini (about 1/4 pound) roll-cut (see page 16)

1   teaspoon sesame oil

¼   cup chopped macadamia nuts

2   tablespoons chopped crystallized ginger

Place a stir-fry pan over high heat until hot. Add the oil, swirling to coat the sides. Add the ginger and cook, stirring, until fragrant, about 20 seconds. Add the squash and broth, reduce the heat to medium, cover, and cook until the squash is half cooked, about 3 minutes. Add the zucchini and continue to cook, covered, until both vegetables are tender, about 3 minutes longer.

Add the sesame oil and toss to coat the vegetables. Stir in the nuts and the crystallized ginger.

Transfer to a serving plate and serve.

BRAISED MUSHROOMS

I visited a small village in Taiwan and was served the freshest shiitake mushrooms that I've ever tasted. They did not even have to remove the stems, as they were tender as well. Serve with Black Pepper Beef (page 148) and Panfried Noodles (page 199) for a complete meal.

½ pound button mushrooms (about 10)
¼ pound oyster mushrooms
¼ pound fresh shiitake mushrooms (about 8)
One 12-ounce can straw mushrooms
2 teaspoons vegetable oil
1 teaspoon butter
2 cloves garlic, minced
⅓ cup water
1½ tablespoons soy sauce
1 teaspoon sugar
⅛ teaspoon black pepper

Trim the base of the stems of the button and oyster mushrooms. Discard the shiitake mushroom stems. Drain the straw mushrooms.

Place a stir-fry pan over high heat until hot. Add the oil and butter and stir until the butter melts. Add the garlic and cook, stirring, until fragrant, about 10 seconds. Add all the mushrooms, the water, soy sauce, sugar, and pepper. Cover and cook until the mushrooms are tender, about 8 minutes.

Transfer to a serving plate and serve.

RUSTIC SMASHED POTATOES

Here's a twist on your mom's mashed potatoes. I used unpeeled red-skinned potatoes. They give the dish a rustic look and pack in extra vitamins from the skins. Serve with Korean-Style Lamb Chops (page 162) and you'll surprise your guests with this colorful side dish.

MAKES 4 TO 6 SERVINGS

2 **pounds red-skinned potatoes,** cut into quarters

1 **teaspoon salt**

³/₄ **cup milk**

1 **tablespoon wasabi powder** mixed with 1¹/₃ tablespoons water

2 **teaspoons chili garlic sauce**

¹/₄ **teaspoon white pepper**

2 **tablespoons butter**

2 **teaspoons sesame oil**

2 **green onions,** thinly sliced

In a large saucepan, combine the potatoes and salt with water to barely cover. Bring to a boil over high heat, reduce the heat to medium, cover, and simmer until the potatoes are tender, about 15 minutes. Drain and return to the pan.

Meanwhile, in a small saucepan, heat the milk over low heat until warm. Add the wasabi paste, chili garlic sauce, and pepper and whisk to blend evenly.

Add the milk mixture to the potatoes and, using a potato masher, mash until the potatoes absorb the liquid. The potatoes should remain lumpy. Add the butter and sesame oil and stir until the butter melts. Garnish with the green onions and serve.

TURMERIC RICE

Your family will be surprised when they see this beautiful yellow rice. Though neutral in flavor, the rice shines like gold. Serve with a curry dish, since turmeric is an ingredient in both curry powder and some curry pastes, or use for making Golden Fried Rice (page 194).

2 cups long-grain rice

3 cups water

1 tablespoon vegetable oil

1½ teaspoons ground turmeric

1½ teaspoons minced garlic

1½ teaspoons sugar

1 teaspoon salt

In a 2-quart saucepan, combine all the ingredients and mix well. Bring to a boil over medium-high heat, reduce the heat to low, and simmer, uncovered, until craterlike holes form on the surface of the rice, about 6 minutes. Cover and continue cooking, undisturbed, until all the water is absorbed, about 10 minutes.

Let the rice stand for 10 minutes, then fluff with a fork and serve.

MAKES 4 TO 6 SERVINGS

SOYBEAN FRIED RICE

Join the soybean craze! Soybeans are an excellent source of protein, soluble fiber, iron, vitamin B, and other essentials. You'll find soybeans in the produce section of some supermarkets and in the frozen-food sections of others, either in the pod or shelled.

MAKES 4 SERVINGS

1 **cup shelled soybeans,** thawed if frozen
2 **teaspoons vegetable oil**
2 **cloves garlic,** minced
4 **cups cold cooked long-grain rice**
2 **tablespoons chicken broth**
1½ **tablespoons oyster-flavored sauce**
2 **eggs, lightly beaten**
2 **teaspoons** *furikake* **or shredded nori**

Bring a small saucepan filled with water to a boil over high heat. Add the soybeans and cook until tender-crisp, about 3 minutes; drain and set aside.

Place a stir-fry pan over high heat until hot. Add the oil, swirling to coat the sides. Add the garlic and cook until fragrant, about 10 seconds. Add the rice, separating the grains with the back of a spoon. Stir in the soybeans and cook until the rice is heated through, 2 to 3 minutes. Add the broth and oyster-flavored sauce and stir to combine. Make a well in the center of the rice, add the eggs, and gently stir the eggs until they form soft curds, about 1 minute. Stir to mix the eggs into the rice.

Transfer to a serving plate, sprinkle with *furikake*, and serve.

FISH FRIED RICE

Feel like something fishy and fun? This goes well with Baked Black-Bean Catfish (page 113), so when you're grocery shopping, buy some extra fish for the fried rice. Round out the meal with Swiss Chard with Black Bean Garlic Sauce (page 183).

MAKES 4 SERVINGS

1 tablespoon vegetable oil

5 ounces firm white fish fillet or sea scallops, cut into small cubes

4 cups cold cooked long-grain rice

1 cup thinly sliced baby bok choy or other leafy green

2 teaspoons fish sauce

2 teaspoons soy sauce

2 tablespoons chopped fresh cilantro

Place a stir-fry pan over high heat until hot. Add the oil, swirling to coat the sides. Add the fish and cook, stirring, until it turns opaque, about 1½ minutes. Add the rice, separating the grains with the back of a spoon. Add the bok choy, fish sauce, and soy sauce and stir to combine. Cook until the rice is heated through, 2 to 3 minutes. Stir in the cilantro, transfer to a serving plate, and serve.

HUE-STYLE FRIED RICE

Over the past few years, I've been lucky enough to travel to the beautiful country of Vietnam. This is one of the many dishes in this book that reflect the flavors of that country's distinctive cuisine.

2 tablespoons sesame seeds

3 tablespoons vegetable oil

1 lemongrass stalk, bottom 4 inches only, minced

2 walnut-sized shallots, coarsely chopped

2 cloves garlic, coarsely chopped

1 red jalapeño chili, chopped

2 teaspoons sugar

1 small yellow onion, coarsely chopped

4 cups cold cooked long-grain rice

2 tablespoons chicken broth

2 tablespoons fish sauce

¼ teaspoon black pepper

8 fresh cilantro sprigs

In a small frying pan, toast the sesame seeds over medium heat, shaking the pan frequently, until lightly colored, 3 to 4 minutes. Immediately pour onto a plate to cool.

In a food processor, combine 1 tablespoon of the oil, lemongrass, shallots, garlic, chili, and sugar. Process to form a paste, scraping down the sides as necessary.

Place a stir-fry pan over medium heat until hot. Add 1 tablespoon of the remaining oil, swirling to coat the sides. Add the lemongrass paste and cook, stirring, until fragrant, about 5 minutes. Remove the paste to a small bowl. Return the stir-fry pan to high heat and add the remaining 1 tablespoon oil, swirling to coat the sides. Add the onion and cook, stirring, until fragrant, about 30 seconds. Add the rice, separating the grains with the back of a spoon. Stir-fry until the rice is heated through and begins to smell toasty, 4 to 5 minutes. Stir in the broth, fish sauce, pepper, and lemongrass paste and cook, stirring, until the liquid is absorbed, about 1 minute. Transfer to a serving plate, garnish with the sesame seeds and cilantro, and serve.

GOLDEN FRIED RICE

This unique side dish, full of wonderful flavors and ingredients, is a great way to use leftover Turmeric Rice. You can use cold cooked long-grain rice as a substitute.

MAKES 4 SERVINGS

2 tablespoons vegetable oil

⅓ cup diced yellow onion

1 tablespoon minced ginger

1 tablespoon minced garlic

2 eggs, lightly beaten

2 Chinese sausages, 2 ounces each, thinly sliced on the diagonal

¼ pound medium-sized raw shrimp, peeled and deveined

3 cups cold cooked Turmeric Rice (page 189) or cooked long-grain rice

1 tablespoon chili garlic sauce

1 tablespoon fish sauce

½ cup pineapple chunks

Place a stir-fry pan over high heat until hot. Add the oil, swirling to coat the sides. Add the onion, ginger, and garlic and cook, stirring, until fragrant, about 15 seconds. Add the eggs, Chinese sausages, and shrimp and cook, without stirring, for 30 seconds to allow the eggs to set slightly. Stir to break up the eggs and then continue cooking until the eggs are firm and the shrimp turn pink, about 2 minutes.

Add the rice, chili garlic sauce, fish sauce, and pineapple chunks and separate the rice grains with the back of a spoon. Stir to combine all the ingredients and cook, stirring, until the rice is heated through, 2 to 3 minutes.

Transfer to a serving plate and serve.

COCONUT RICE

Who said rice was boring? Add a touch of the tropics and rice will never be boring again. Be sure not to shake the can of coconut milk before you open it. For this recipe, only the milk is needed. The cream will make the dish much too rich and interfere with the cooking time. Open the unshaken can, spoon off the layer of cream on top and reserve it for another use, and measure out the amount of milk you need.

MAKES 4 SERVINGS

¼ cup unsweetened flaked coconut

⅔ cup unsweetened coconut milk, cream spooned off and saved for another use

1⅓ cups water

1 cup long-grain rice

1 tablespoon minced ginger

½ teaspoon salt

In a small frying pan, toast the coconut over medium heat, stirring frequently, until lightly browned, 3 to 4 minutes. Immediately pour onto a plate to cool. Set aside.

In a 2-quart pan, combine the coconut milk, water, rice, ginger, and salt. Bring to a boil over high heat, reduce the heat to low, and simmer, uncovered, until craterlike holes form on the surface of the rice, about 6 minutes. Cover and continue cooking, undisturbed, until all the liquid is absorbed, about 10 minutes.

Fluff the rice with a fork. Transfer to a serving platter, sprinkle with the toasted coconut, and serve.

CARROT-PINEAPPLE RICE

Serve with Glazed Grilled Pork Chops (page 168) and Almond Baby Bok Choy (page 177) for a complete dinner.

One 8-ounce can crushed pineapple, in natural juice

1⅓ cups water

1 carrot, peeled and grated (about ½ cup)

1 cup long-grain rice

½ teaspoon salt

3 green onions, thinly sliced on the diagonal

½ teaspoon sesame oil

Drain the pineapple, reserving the juice. Pour the juice into a 2-quart pan. Add the water, carrot, rice, and salt and bring to a boil over high heat. Reduce the heat to medium and simmer, uncovered, until craterlike holes form on the surface of the rice, about 6 minutes. Reduce the heat to low, cover, and cook, undisturbed, until all the liquid is absorbed, about 10 minutes.

Fluff the rice with a fork and stir in the pineapple, green onions, and sesame oil. Cover until ready to serve.

MAKES 4 SERVINGS

EIGHT PRECIOUS FRIED RICE

Don't be distracted or deterred by the long list of ingredients. This dish is a delicious combination of rice, nuts, vegetables, dried fruit, and a touch of meat. Despite the name, more than eight items are added to this fried rice, but when a Chinese dish is called "eight precious," you know it has many delicious flavors and interesting textures. The number eight symbolizes good luck in Chinese culture.

MAKES 4 SERVINGS

2 tablespoons vegetable oil

2 cloves garlic, minced

2 teaspoons oolong tea leaves

1 cup diced cooked meat such as smoked ham or roasted duck

¼ cup pine nuts

1 cup shredded napa cabbage

½ cup chopped cauliflower florets

½ cup diced Chinese long beans or green beans

1 egg, lightly beaten

5 cups cold cooked long-grain rice

½ cup canned or thawed, frozen corn

¼ cup golden raisins

¼ cup dried cranberries

3 tablespoons vegetable broth

2 tablespoons oyster-flavored sauce

½ teaspoon salt

⅛ teaspoon white pepper

Place a stir-fry pan over medium-high heat until hot. Add the oil, swirling to coat the sides. Add the garlic and tea leaves and cook, stirring, until fragrant, about 20 seconds. Add the meat, pine nuts, napa cabbage, cauliflower, and beans and cook, stirring, until the vegetables are tender-crisp, about 2½ minutes. Add the egg and cook, lightly stirring, until the egg begins to set, about 1 minute. Add the rice, separating the grains with the back of a spoon. Add the corn, raisins, cranberries, broth, oyster-flavored sauce, salt, and pepper and mix well. Cook, stirring, until the rice is heated through, 2 to 3 minutes.

Transfer to a serving plate and serve.

PANFRIED NOODLES

The key to preparing the perfect crispy noodle pancake is the swirling of the noodles in the pan. This keeps them from sticking. Crispy noodles complement a variety of stir-fries, including Black Pepper Beef (page 148) and Singapore Velvet Shrimp (page 103). Cooked dried pasta can be substituted for the fresh Chinese egg noodles.

16 ounces fresh Chinese egg noodles
 1 teaspoon sesame oil
 2 tablespoons vegetable oil

Bring a large pot filled with water to a boil over high heat. Add the noodles and cook according to the package directions. Drain, rinse with cold water, and drain again. Return the noodles to the pot and toss with the sesame oil.

Place a wide, nonstick frying pan over medium heat until hot. Add 1 tablespoon of the vegetable oil, swirling to coat the bottom. Spread half of the noodles (about 2 cups) evenly in the pan. Cook, turning once, until the noodles are golden brown, about 5 minutes on each side. As the noodles cook, swirl the pan once or twice to prevent the noodles from sticking. Transfer the noodle pancake to a large, heatproof serving platter and keep warm in a 200°F oven. Cook the remaining noodles in the same way, using the remaining 1 tablespoon oil.

Serve topped with a stir-fry.

MAKES 2 NOODLE PANCAKES

SPICY SOBA NOODLES

Japanese soba noodles, made from buckwheat flour and wheat flour, are treated to a spicy dressing here. This is a great dish for a potluck dinner. It goes well with a variety of grill items or with something as simple as Peppery Chicken Wings (page 55).

MAKES 4 SERVINGS

8   ounces dried soba noodles
2   cups sliced napa cabbage
½   teaspoon sesame oil

Dressing
2   tablespoons vegetable oil
2   tablespoons fresh lemon juice
2   teaspoons soy sauce
1½ teaspoons sweet chili sauce
1   teaspoon ground turmeric
1   teaspoon grated ginger

¼   cup sliced pickled ginger
2   tablespoons chopped fresh cilantro
2   green onions, julienned

Bring a large pot filled with water to a boil over high heat. Add the noodles and cook according to the package directions. Drain, rinse with cold water, and drain again. Place the noodles in a large bowl, add the napa cabbage and sesame oil, and toss to mix evenly. To make the dressing, combine all the ingredients in a bowl and mix well. Pour the dressing over the noodle mixture and add the pickled ginger, cilantro, and green onions. Toss to coat evenly. Serve immediately, or cover and refrigerate for up to 3 hours.

COLD TEA SOMEN NOODLES

This is another way to enjoy tea. Oolong tea adds a subtle layer of flavor to the dish. Somen noodles are thin, white Japanese noodles, but soba noodles, made from buckwheat flour, can be used in their place.

MAKES 4 SERVINGS

6 cups water

6 bags oolong tea

8 ounces dried somen noodles

1½ teaspoons sesame oil

¾ cup shredded carrot

1 cup bean sprouts

½ cup julienned smoked ham

Dressing

2 teaspoons sesame seeds

2 tablespoons soy sauce

2 teaspoons sesame oil

1 teaspoon wasabi paste

½ teaspoon sugar

1 sheet nori, cut into narrow strips

In a large pot, bring the water to a boil. Turn off the heat, add the tea bags, and let steep for 2 minutes. Remove ¼ cup of the tea and set aside for the dressing. Remove the tea bags and discard. Bring the remaining tea to a boil, add the noodles, and cook according to the package directions. Drain, rinse with cold water, and drain again. Return the noodles to the pot, add the sesame oil, and toss to coat. Add the carrot, bean sprouts, and ham and toss to mix. Transfer to a serving plate, cover, and refrigerate until ready to serve.

To make the dressing, place the sesame seeds in a small frying pan over medium heat. Toast, shaking the pan frequently, until lightly browned, 3 to 4 minutes. Immediately pour into a small bowl to cool. Add the ¼ cup reserved tea, soy sauce, sesame oil, wasabi paste, and sugar and mix well.

Just before serving, pour the dressing over the noodles and toss to mix. Garnish with the nori and serve.

YAN CAN LO MEIN

If Yan can make this *lo mein*, you can, too! Although fresh Chinese noodles have the best texture for a stir-fried dish, spaghetti or angel hair pasta can be used if you can't find them. Add ¼ pound cubed tofu, chicken, or shrimp for a more substantial meal.

MAKES 4 SERVINGS

8 **ounces fresh Chinese egg noodles**

1 **tablespoon vegetable oil**

2 **cloves garlic,** minced

1 **cup shredded carrot**

2 **celery stalks,** julienned

2 **cups bean sprouts**

½ **cup snow peas,** ends trimmed and cut in half on the diagonal

½ **cup julienned bamboo shoots**

2 **green onions,** thinly sliced

2 **tablespoons oyster-flavored sauce**

1 **teaspoon sesame oil**

Bring a large pot filled with water to a boil over high heat. Add the noodles and cook according to package directions. Drain, rinse with cold water, and drain again.

Place a stir-fry pan over high heat until hot. Add the vegetable oil, swirling to coat the sides. Add the garlic and cook, stirring, until fragrant, about 10 seconds. Add the carrot, celery, bean sprouts, snow peas, bamboo shoots, and green onions and stir-fry until the vegetables wilt slightly, about 2 minutes. Add the noodles, oyster-flavored sauce, and sesame oil and toss to mix the noodles with the vegetables. Cook, stirring, until all the vegetables are tender, about 2 minutes. Transfer to a serving plate and serve.

SIMPLE SESAME NOODLES

This easy, flavorful dish can be made ahead of time and eaten warm, chilled, or at room temperature. What a versatile main course!

2 tablespoons sesame seeds

8 ounces fresh Chinese egg noodles

1 teaspoon sesame oil

Sauce

¼ cup chicken broth

2 tablespoons soy sauce

2 teaspoons sesame oil

2 teaspoons vegetable oil

½ yellow onion, thinly sliced

2 cups shredded napa cabbage or green head cabbage

1 cup bean sprouts

½ cup shredded carrot

¼ cup packed fresh cilantro leaves

In a small frying pan, toast the sesame seeds over medium heat, shaking the pan frequently, until lightly colored, 3 to 4 minutes. Immediately pour onto a plate to cool. Set aside for garnish.

Bring a large pot filled with water to a boil over high heat. Add the noodles and cook according to package directions. Drain, rinse with cold water, and drain again. Place the noodles in a large bowl, add the 1 teaspoon sesame oil, and stir to coat.

To make the sauce, combine all the ingredients in a small bowl and mix well.

Place a stir-fry pan over high heat until hot. Add the vegetable oil, swirling to coat the sides. Add the onion and cook, stirring, until it begins to wilt and is fragrant, about 1 minute. Add the cabbage, bean sprouts, and carrot and stir-fry until the cabbage is tender-crisp, about 2 ½ minutes. Add the sauce and noodles and toss until all the ingredients are evenly distributed.

Transfer to a serving plate, garnish with the sesame seeds and cilantro, and serve.

HAKKA VEGETARIAN CHOW FUN

The Hakka people traveled from their native China to many Asian countries. These gypsies brought their food and culture wherever they went. Hakka cuisine is known for its simplicity, but that doesn't mean it's not delicious. Chinese celery, which has long, slender, hollow stems topped with flat leaves that resemble cilantro, has a very strong celery flavor. You can use regular celery in its place, but throw a few stems of cilantro in for extra flavor.

2 dried black mushrooms

12 ounces fresh or 8 ounces dried flat rice noodles, about ¼ inch wide

Sauce

½ cup vegetable broth

2 tablespoons soy sauce

½ teaspoon sugar

2 ½ tablespoons vegetable oil

2 cloves garlic, minced

1 teaspoon minced ginger

1 cup shredded napa cabbage

¾ cup shredded carrot

¾ cup bean sprouts

½ cup chopped Chinese celery, or 1 small regular celery stalk, julienned

¼ cup sliced Sichuan preserved vegetable or mild kimchee (optional)

3 green onions, cut into 1-inch lengths

1 egg, lightly beaten

MAKES 4 SERVINGS

In a bowl, soak the mushrooms in warm water to cover until softened, about 15 minutes; drain. Discard the stems and thinly slice the caps. Set aside.

If using dried rice noodles, soak in warm water to cover until softened, about 15 minutes; drain. If using fresh noodles, separate them by pulling them apart.

To make the sauce, combine all the ingredients in a small bowl and stir until the sugar dissolves. Place a stir-fry pan over high heat until hot. Add 2 tablespoons of the oil, swirling to coat the sides. Add the noodles and stir-fry for 1 minute. Add half of the sauce and stir to coat the noodles. Remove the noodles from the pan. Return the stir-fry pan to high heat until hot. Add the remaining ½ tablespoon oil, swirling to coat the sides. Add the garlic and ginger and cook, stirring, until fragrant, about 30 seconds. Add the remaining ingredients except the egg, and stir-fry until the vegetables are tender-crisp, about 2 minutes. Push the vegetables to the side of pan, add the egg, and stir-fry until the egg is cooked, about 1 minute. Return the noodles to the pan and toss gently. Add the remaining sauce, stir to coat evenly, and cook for 2 minutes. Serve.

HAIHAN FUN MEIN

This is a perfect dish for using up leftover noodles. That's what I do! The combination of rice noodles *(fun)* and egg noodles *(mein)* makes it interesting. If your egg noodles are yellow, the contrast is appealing. Use any meat or seafood that you have in your refrigerator. I like to add a link of Chinese sausage.

MAKES 4 SERVINGS

¼ **pound boneless, skinless chicken breast or thigh meat,** cut into 1-inch pieces

¼ **pound medium-sized raw shrimp,** peeled and deveined

1 **teaspoon cornstarch**

2 **teaspoons oyster-flavored sauce**

Sauce

1 **cup chicken broth**

3 **tablespoons oyster-flavored sauce**

1 **tablespoon sweet chili sauce**

1 **tablespoon vegetable oil**

2 **cloves garlic,** minced

1 **walnut-sized shallot,** thinly sliced

1 **red jalapeño chili,** thinly sliced

1 **celery stalk,** thinly sliced on the diagonal

2 **cups cooked rice stick noodles**

1½ **cups cooked Chinese egg noodles**

1 **egg,** lightly beaten

1 **teaspoon sesame oil**

In a bowl, combine the chicken, shrimp, cornstarch, and oyster-flavored sauce and stir to coat. Let stand for 10 minutes.

To make the sauce, combine all the ingredients in a small bowl and mix well.

Heat a stir-fry pan over high heat until hot. Add the vegetable oil, swirling to coat the sides. Add the garlic, shallot, and chili and cook, stirring, until fragrant, about 30 seconds. Add the chicken and shrimp, stir-fry until the shrimp begin to curl and turn pink, about 2 minutes. Add the celery and stir-fry for 1 minute.

Add the noodles and sauce and cook, stirring gently, until the chicken is no longer pink and the noodles are heated through, about 2 minutes. Push the noodles toward the sides of the pan and pour the egg into the center. Cook until the egg is almost set, about 1 minute. Sprinkle with the sesame oil and toss to mix the egg into the noodles.

Transfer to a serving plate and serve.

GARLICKY PEANUT NOODLES

Serve this versatile dish hot or at room temperature with Grilled Satay Chicken Tenders (page 141) or Quick Char Siu (page 169). For a vegetarian main course, toss the dressed noodles with a thinly sliced cucumber, carrot, and a few handfuls of bean sprouts for extra crunch. The noodles can be tossed in the dressing up to a day before serving.

MAKES 6 TO 8 SERVINGS

Peanut Dressing

- ¼ cup rice vinegar
- 2 tablespoons fresh lemon juice
- 2 tablespoons soy sauce
- ⅓ cup smooth peanut butter
- 1 tablespoon chili garlic sauce
- 2 tablespoons packed brown sugar
- 2 cloves garlic, minced

- 16 ounces fresh Chinese egg noodles
- ⅓ cup chopped fresh cilantro
- 2 green onions, thinly sliced
- ¼ cup chopped roasted peanuts

To make the dressing, combine all the ingredients in a blender and whirl until smooth. Set aside.

Bring a large pot filled with water to a boil over high heat. Add the noodles and cook according to the package directions. Drain, rinse with cold water, and drain again.

Place the noodles in a large bowl with the cilantro and green onions. Pour the dressing over the noodles and toss to coat evenly. Sprinkle the peanuts over the top. Serve hot or at room temperature.

DESSERTS & DRINKS

TROPICAL FRUIT WITH LEMON-GINGER SYRUP

Because this syrup complements so many kinds of fruit, I keep a jar of it in the refrigerator for as long as a month. Don't limit its use to tropical fruit. It goes nicely with fresh apricots, peaches, pears, and plums, too.

MAKES 6 SERVINGS

Syrup

- 2 **cups sugar**
- 1 **cup water**
- 1 **lemon, thinly sliced**
- 6 **quarter-sized slices ginger,** lightly crushed
- 3 **whole star anise**

- 1 **papaya,** peeled, halved, seeded, and cut into cubes
- 1 **mango,** peeled, pitted, and cut into cubes
- 1 **banana,** peeled and sliced
- 3 **kiwifruits,** peeled and cut into wedges
- 1 **tablespoon chopped crystallized ginger**
     Vanilla ice cream for serving (optional)

To make the syrup, combine all the ingredients in a saucepan. Cook over low heat, stirring occasionally, until the sugar dissolves. Simmer for 5 minutes longer to infuse the flavors. Let the syrup cool, then strain and discard the solids. Chill until ready to use.

In a bowl, combine the papaya, mango, banana, kiwifruits, and ginger. Drizzle about 1 cup of the syrup over the fruit and stir gently to coat evenly.

Serve chilled, alone or with a scoop of ice cream.

COCONUT CUSTARD

Some people consider custard nursery food, but they haven't tasted one made with a double dose of coconut. Rich and velvety, it makes a splendid dessert to end a dinner party. Look for unsweetened flaked coconut among the bulk items in a good supermarket, or you can find it in a natural-foods store or an Indian market.

MAKES 4 SERVINGS

2/3 cup unsweetened flaked coconut

4 large eggs

One 13 1/2-ounce can unsweetened coconut milk

1/2 cup sugar

Place a nonstick frying pan over medium-high heat until hot. Add the coconut and toast, stirring, until lightly browned, about 2 minutes. Immediately pour onto a plate to cool.

In a blender, combine the eggs, coconut milk, 1/3 cup of the toasted coconut, and the sugar. Blend briefly to combine. Pour the mixture into a glass pie dish and cover the dish with plastic wrap.

Prepare a stir-fry pan for steaming (see page 16). Place the dish in the stir-fry pan, cover, and steam over medium heat until the custard is set, 20 to 25 minutes.

Carefully remove the dish from the steamer and discard the plastic wrap. Sprinkle the remaining 1/3 cup toasted coconut over the top. Scoop into bowls and serve warm.

SWEET PEANUT DESSERT SOUP

A savory soup is part of most Chinese meals, but it is also not uncommon to find a sweet soup served for dessert. It can be made from mung beans, tapioca, red beans, lotus seeds, walnuts, or, of course, peanuts. Served warm, a sweet soup is a classic finale to a festive Chinese meal. Serve with Twin-Ginger Shortbread Cookies (page 216).

3/4 cup chunky peanut butter

3 1/2 cups water

1/4 cup chopped unsalted peanuts

1/4 cup packed brown sugar

One 6-ounce can evaporated milk

1 tablespoon cornstarch dissolved in 2 tablespoons water

Place the peanut butter in a saucepan. Add the water, in batches, stirring after each addition until the mixture is smooth. Stir in the peanuts and brown sugar. Bring to a boil over medium-high heat, reduce the heat to low, and simmer, stirring once or twice, until it reduces slightly, about 15 minutes. Add the evaporated milk and cornstarch solution and cook, stirring, until the soup thickens slightly, about 1 minute.

Ladle into bowls and serve.

MAKES 4 TO 6 SERVINGS

TWIN-GINGER SHORTBREAD COOKIES

If you love ginger, you will love these cookies! I have added fresh and crystallized ginger to a rich shortbread recipe. For extra crunch, I used chopped glazed walnuts, but regular walnuts can be used in their place.

MAKES ABOUT 2
DOZEN COOKIES

1 cup unsalted butter (2 sticks), at room temperature

½ cup sugar

⅓ cup chopped crystallized ginger

1 tablespoon grated ginger

½ cup chopped purchased glazed walnuts

2 cups all-purpose flour

¼ teaspoon salt

Preheat the oven to 350°F.

In a large bowl, using an electric mixer on high speed, beat together the butter and sugar until light and fluffy, about 2 minutes.

Add the crystallized ginger, grated ginger, and glazed walnuts and mix until incorporated. Add the flour and salt and mix on low speed until the mixture forms a dough.

Using your hands, shape the dough into $1\frac{1}{3}$-inch balls and place them 2 inches apart on an ungreased baking sheet. Using your fingers, press the balls into $\frac{1}{3}$-inch-thick circles.

Bake the cookies until lightly browned, about 20 minutes. Let cool on the baking sheet for 5 minutes, then transfer to a rack and let cool completely. Store in an airtight container; they will keep for up to 2 weeks.

FIVE-SPICE PINEAPPLE BANANA SPLIT

Here, Asian ingredients update a soda fountain classic, and glazed walnuts provide the crowning touch. You'll find them in the baking aisle or in the snack and nuts section of the supermarket.

MAKES 4 SERVINGS

Pineapple Topping

One 8-ounce can crushed pineapple, in natural juice, undrained

¼ cup water

1 tablespoon sugar

1 teaspoon grated ginger

¼ teaspoon Chinese five-spice powder

3 bananas, peeled and quartered lengthwise

1 pint vanilla or coconut ice cream

⅓ cup purchased chocolate syrup

⅓ cup Zippy Ginger Syrup (page 39)

Whipped cream for serving

½ cup purchased glazed walnuts

To make the pineapple topping, combine all the ingredients in a small saucepan. Place over medium heat and cook, stirring occasionally, until the sugar dissolves and the syrup thickens slightly, about 5 minutes.

To assemble the desserts: Divide the bananas among 4 bowls. Top each one with 1 scoop of ice cream, one-fourth of the warm pineapple topping, a few tablespoons of the chocolate and ginger syrups, and a dollop of whipped cream. Top each dessert with one-fourth of the glazed walnuts and serve.

SPICED BANANA ROLLS

Soft spiced banana, crisp wonton wrap, warm chocolate-ginger sauce, and cool ice cream make for a wonderful study in contrasts. This dessert looks beautiful in the bowl and tastes heavenly

MAKES 4 SERVINGS

3 medium-firm bananas

2 tablespoons packed light brown sugar

½ teaspoon Chinese five-spice powder

12 wonton wrappers

Vegetable oil for deep-frying

½ cup purchased chocolate syrup

¼ cup Zippy Ginger Syrup (page 39)

1 pint vanilla ice cream

Peel the bananas, halve them lengthwise, and then halve crosswise. Place in a bowl with the brown sugar and five-spice powder and stir gently to coat evenly.

To make each roll: Place a wonton wrapper on a work surface. Place a piece of banana diagonally across the center of the wrapper. Brush the edges of the wrapper with water, roll up the banana inside the wrapper, and press to seal. The ends of the roll will be open. Pour oil to a depth of 2 inches into a 2-quart saucepan and heat to 350°F on a deep-frying thermometer. Add the rolls, a few at a time, and deep-fry, turning once, until golden brown, about 1 minute one each side. Remove with a slotted spoon and drain on paper towels.

In a small saucepan, combine the chocolate syrup and ginger syrup and bring to a simmer over medium heat. Remove from the heat.

To assemble each dessert: Place a scoop of ice cream in a bowl, top with 3 banana rolls, and drizzle one-fourth of the chocolate-ginger syrup over the top.

ASIAN PEAR CRUMBLE

A crumble is as much a part of the American food tradition as pie is, but it is much faster to put together. I've given this all-American dessert an Asian accent by using Asian pears and Chinese five-spice powder. It is especially delicious served warm with vanilla ice cream or lightly whipped cream.

MAKES 6 SERVINGS

½ cup dried cranberries
1½ pounds Asian pears, peeled, cored, and thinly sliced
1 lemon
½ teaspoon Chinese five-spice powder
1 cup water
2 bags jasmine tea
1 tablespoon packed brown sugar
3 tablespoons apricot-pineapple preserves
1 teaspoon cornstarch dissolved in 2 teaspoons water

Topping

4 tablespoons unsalted butter
¾ cup chopped walnuts
1 tablespoon packed brown sugar
¼ teaspoon Chinese five-spice powder
1 cup panko

Preheat the oven to 350°F.

In a bowl, soak the cranberries in hot water to cover until softened, about 10 minutes; drain. Place the cranberries and pears in a 1⅓-quart casserole. Grate the lemon zest, then juice the lemon. Add the zest, juice, and five-spice powder to the fruit and stir to coat.

In a small saucepan, bring the water to a boil. Remove from the heat, add the tea bags, and let steep for 3 minutes. Discard the tea bags. Add the brown sugar and preserves to the tea and return the pan to medium-high heat. Cook, stirring, until the sugar dissolves and the preserves are melted, about 3 minutes. Increase the heat to high, add the cornstarch solution, and cook, stirring, until the mixture boils and thickens, about 30 seconds. Pour over the fruit.

To make the topping, in a wide frying pan, melt the butter over medium-high heat. Add the nuts and cook, stirring, until they begin to brown, 2 to 3 minutes. Add the brown sugar and five-spice powder and cook until the sugar dissolves. Add the panko and stir to coat. Spoon the topping over the fruit. Bake, uncovered, until the pears are tender and the topping is golden brown, 25 to 30 minutes. Scoop into bowls and serve warm.

CARAMELIZED ASIAN PEARS OVER COCONUT ICE CREAM

Everyone likes ice cream, and there's no easier dessert to serve. Top it with a warm spiced fruit sauce, such as this quickly made Asian pear sauce, and both the diners and the cook will be pleased.

- 4 tablespoons unsalted butter
- ¼ cup packed brown sugar
- ¼ teaspoon Chinese five-spice powder
- 2 Asian pears, peeled, cored, and thinly sliced
- ¼ cup light rum
- 1 pint coconut ice cream

Place a wide frying pan over medium heat until hot. Add the butter, brown sugar, and five-spice powder and cook, stirring occasionally, until the sugar dissolves. Increase the heat to high, add the pears, and cook until tender, about 2 minutes. Remove the pan from the heat and pour in the rum. Return the pan to high heat and carefully ignite the rum with a match. (Do not do this beneath an exhaust fan or near flammable items.) Reduce the heat to medium-high and cook for another 2 minutes.

Scoop the ice cream into 4 bowls and spoon the warm sauce over the top.

MAKES 4 SERVINGS

SWEET COCONUT RICE
WITH CARAMELIZED PINEAPPLE

This is an Asian version of rice pudding, made the Chinese way with glutinous rice and served with caramelized pineapple. If you don't want to cut up a fresh pineapple, look for precut spears, slices, or chunks in your supermarket produce section.

Sweet Coconut Rice

- 1 cup sweetened condensed milk
- One 13½-ounce can unsweetened coconut milk
- ½ cup sweetened flaked coconut
- 4 cups cooked Quick Glutinous Rice (page 33)

- ½ cup sweetened flaked coconut

Caramelized Pineapple

- 1 pineapple
- ½ cup packed light brown sugar

Fresh mint sprigs for garnish

Preheat the oven to 350°F.

While the oven is heating, make the sweet coconut rice: In a 2-quart saucepan, combine the condensed milk, coconut milk, and ½ cup of coconut and bring to a boil over medium-high heat. Reduce the heat to low and simmer, stirring once or twice, for 5 minutes. Add the glutinous rice and stir until it is moistened. Remove from the heat, cover, and set aside. Spread the second ½ cup of coconut in a pie pan and toast in the oven, stirring frequently, until lightly browned, 4 to 5 minutes. Pour onto a plate to cool. Turn the oven to broil.

To make the caramelized pineapple, use a heavy, sharp knife to cut off the crown from the pineapple, then cut off the shell. Cut the pineapple lengthwise into quarters. Trim away the core from each quarter, and then cut each quarter into 3 wedges. Place in a large bowl, sprinkle with the brown sugar, and toss to coat evenly. Spread the pineapple on an aluminum foil-lined rimmed baking sheet. Slip the pineapple under the broiler 3 to 4 inches from the heat and broil, turning once, until the sugar melts but does not burn, about 2 minutes on each side.

To serve, scoop the rice into bowls and serve with the pineapple wedges. Sprinkle with toasted coconut and garnish with mint.

LEMONGRASS ICED TEA

I enjoy relaxing with this drink. The light, lovely flavor of lemongrass is the perfect citrus accent to green tea.

MAKES 4 OR 5 SERVINGS

5   lemongrass stalks

4   cups water

3   bags green tea

    Sugar

    Ice cubes

    Lemon wedges for garnish

Coarsely chop the bottom 4 inches of the lemongrass stalks. Trim the tops, remove the outside leaves, and save for garnish.

In a small saucepan, bring the water to a boil. Add the tea bags and chopped lemongrass, remove from the heat and let steep for 10 minutes. Strain, sweeten to taste with sugar, and then refrigerate until ready to serve.

Fill tall chilled glasses with ice and pour the tea over the ice. Garnish each glass with a lemongrass top and a lemon wedge.

ZIPPY GINGER FLOAT

Any kid, or kid-at-heart, will love this fun drink reminiscent of a root beer float.

MAKES 1 SERVING

1   cup club soda

2   tablespoons Zippy Ginger Syrup (page 39)

1   scoop vanilla ice cream

In a tall glass, combine the club soda and ginger syrup and stir to combine. Add the scoop of ice cream. Serve with a spoon and a straw.

Right to Left: Lychee Lemonade, page 229; Lemongrass Iced Tea; Ho Chi Mojito, page 226

ORANGE-PINEAPPLE COOLER

There's no dicing or mincing involved in this healthful drink. Just slice the ginger, drop it into a blender with the juices, and let the appliance do the work. It's a tasty and easy way to get your vitamin C.

MAKES 6 SERVINGS

2 cups fresh orange juice

One 16-ounce can pineapple chunks, in natural juice

6 quarter-sized slices ginger

Ice cubes

3 cups club soda

1 orange, cut into wedges

In a blender, combine the orange juice, pineapple with its juice, and ginger. Whirl until smooth. Put 3 or 4 ice cubes into each of 6 tall glasses, and pour ½ cup of the club soda into each glass. Fill the glasses with the orange-pineapple mixture, dividing it evenly, and garnish each glass with an orange wedge.

HO CHI MOJITO

This refreshing mix of citrus juices is a perfect cocktail for a warm afternoon (see photograph, page 225). When I have a moment to relax, a glass of this hits the spot.

MAKES 2 SERVINGS

10 fresh mint leaves

2 tablespoons Zippy Ginger Syrup (page 39)

¼ cup light rum

Juice of ½ orange (about ¼ cup)

Juice of ½ lime (about 1 tablespoon)

Juice of ½ lemon (about 2 tablespoons)

Ice cubes

Club soda

2 orange slices

Divide the mint leaves between 2 tall glasses. Pour I tablespoon of the ginger syrup into each glass. With the handle of a long wooden spoon, gently bruise the mint leaves. Divide the rum, orange juice, lime juice, and lemon juice evenly between the glasses, then add ice cubes and a splash of club soda to each glass. Stir to blend and garnish each glass with an orange slice.

REFRESHING BEER DRINK

When you want to serve a light alcoholic beverage that is a thirst quencher, try this. I use Tsing Tao beer from China, but any light pilsner will work. If you have a jalapeño chili on hand, add a thin slice or two for an extra kick.

2	tablespoons fresh lime juice
2	tablespoons superfine sugar
	About 1 cup crushed ice
One	12-ounce bottle light pilsner

Divide the lime juice and sugar between 2 tall glasses and stir until the sugar dissolves. Add $1/3$ cup of the crushed ice to each glass, then fill with the beer.

MAKES 2 SERVINGS

PAPAYA COCKTAIL

Whether it is a pool party or a holiday party, this cocktail will turn the occasion into a special event. Look in the juice aisle of the supermarket for different fruit nectars, such as guava and passion fruit, to use in place of the papaya nectar.

1	**papaya,** peeled, halved, seeded, and cut into chunks
1	cup pineapple juice
$1/4$	cup fresh lime juice (about 2 limes)
$1/4$	cup honey
1	tablespoon chopped ginger
$1\frac{1}{2}$	cups papaya nectar
2	cups ginger ale
1	cup light rum
	Ice cubes

In a blender, combine the papaya, pineapple juice, lime juice, honey, and ginger. Whirl until smooth. Pour into a large pitcher and add the papaya nectar, ginger ale, and rum. Stir lightly to mix. Fill 6 tall glasses with ice cubes, pour in the fruit mixture, and serve with a straw.

MAKES 6 SERVINGS

PEKING SUN COCKTAIL

On a special occasion, toast a loved one with this colorful cocktail.

MAKES 2 SERVINGS

½ cup fresh orange juice
¼ cup cranberry juice cocktail
¼ cup vodka
¼ cup club soda
1 teaspoon Zippy Ginger Syrup (page 39)
Crushed ice
2 orange slices

In a pitcher, combine the orange juice, cranberry juice cocktail, vodka, club soda, and ginger syrup. Fill 2 tall glasses half full with crushed ice. Pour the cocktail over the ice and garnish each glass with an orange slice.

GUAVA BELLINI

Here's something to enjoy at New Year's celebrations, but this effervescent drink is a good choice for any festive occasion.

MAKES 6 SERVINGS

One 12-ounce can guava nectar or juice or mango juice, well chilled
One 750-ml bottle brut-style sparkling wine, well chilled

Pour about ¼ cup guava nectar into each of 6 chilled champagne flutes. This should fill each glass about one-third full. Fill the remaining two-thirds of each glass with sparkling wine.

CREAMY FRUIT SHAKE

For speed and ease, look for frozen mango chunks sold in 1½-pound bags. The chunks are individually frozen, so you can scoop out as many as you need. Make this shake different each time: use kiwifruit, passion fruit, or even peaches in place of the mango.

One 14-ounce can sweetened condensed milk
1 cup diced, peeled mango (1 small mango)
2 bananas, peeled and sliced
4 large fresh mint leaves
2 cups ice cubes
4 fresh mint sprigs

In a blender, combine the condensed milk, mango, bananas, and mint leaves. Whirl until smooth. Add the ice and blend until slushy. Divide among 4 tall glasses and garnish each glass with a mint sprig.

MAKES 4 SERVINGS

LYCHEE LEMONADE

You can keep this make-ahead lemonade base in the refrigerator for up to a week. To make an individual slushy, whirl ²/₃ cup of the base with 3 or 4 ice cubes. If a party is in your plans, you could double this recipe and serve the lemonade base in a punch bowl over a block of ice. (See photograph, page 225.)

One 20-ounce can lychees, with syrup
One 12-ounce can frozen lemonade concentrate
2½ cups water
Ice cubes
1 lemon, thinly sliced
5 fresh mint sprigs

In a blender, combine the lychees and their syrup, lemonade concentrate, and water. Whirl until smooth. Fill 5 tall chilled glasses with ice and pour the lemonade over the ice. Garnish each glass with a lemon slice and a mint sprig.

MAKES 5 SERVINGS

有緣君士
點醒沉睡英雄
指引迷途君子
五行故内見榮枯
八字命含分貴賤
何不下馬問前程
若感人生多障碍
緣
HELP YOU LOOK YOUR FORTUNE
HUNDRED PERCENT TRUE I'M SPEAK
ENGLISH TRUST ME 35 YEARS JOB
前程萬里
旺丁旺財
驅鬼鎮宅
辟邪治鬼
二胡洋琴
教授乐器
代寫书信
指点迷津
婚姻配
掌紋氣色
紅課择白
八字算命
看宅風水
值年太岁符、平安符、辟邪治鬼鎮宅灵符.
TEL 212-343-9878

QUICK & EASY MEAL SUGGESTIONS

When deciding what's for dinner, I take five things into consideration:

1. How much time do I have?
2. Who is coming to dinner?
3. What is in my refrigerator?
4. Will the meal involve only a quick trip to the store?
5. What cooking methods am I going to use so everything will be ready at the same time?

It is generally best to have some variety on the dinner table, which is achieved by pulling together a combination of dishes. A good rule of thumb is to have one main dish and two side dishes. There are exceptions to that rule, however. Some hearty main dishes may only need one simple side dish. Or, a substantial soup can be the main course served with only one vegetable side dish and a dessert. You might also opt for one dish that has it all, which is known as a one-dish meal. The menu possibilities are endless, but I've put together some complete meal ideas that I enjoy. Give them a try and then create your own.

A SOUP AND A QUICK STIR-FRY

What a perfect combination! Simply add a bowl of steamed rice for a hearty meal. All of these meals can be made in less than half an hour. Start cooking the rice first, put the soup on the stove, and finish off with the stir-fry. Everything will arrive at the table at the same time.

Miso Soup and Shrimp and Sugar Snap Peas Stir-fry

Crab and Asparagus Soup and Lemon-Pepper Beef

Creamy Mushroom Soup and Three-Alarm Firecracker Chicken

Coconut Squash Soup and Sichuan Garlic Lamb

TWO PANS ONLY

With these two dishes, everything you need will be on the table.

Rice Cooker Chicken and Mushrooms and Simply Gai Lan

Vegetable and Tofu Green Curry and Steamed White Rice

Wok-Tossed Pork with Miso Glaze and Soybean Fried Rice

Poached Halibut over Soba Noodles and Ginger Sugar Snap Peas

Grilled Satay Chicken Tenders and Hakka Vegetarian Chow Fun

Pineapple Hot-and-Sour Soup and Grilled Beef Vietnamese Street Sandwich

Curried Coconut Potpie and green salad with Asian Vinaigrette

JUST ADD RICE

All you need alongside these tasty dishes is a bowl of steamed rice and the meal is complete.
Baked Black-Bean Catfish and Swiss Chard with Black Bean Garlic Sauce

Bold Basil Beef and Flash-Fried Asparagus and Long Beans

Simple Steamed Tofu and Eggplant in Plum Sauce

Fish and Long Bean Stir-fry and Coconut Custard

Steamed Fish with Lemongrass Oil

ONE-DISH MEALS

Everything you need is in one bowl.

Monday-Night Dumpling Soup

Grilled Salmon Sushi Rice-Bowl

Chili-Braised Beef Noodle Bowl

CAN SALAD BE A MEAL?

Well, of course! Salads are not common on everyday Asian tables, but my family loves them, and I enjoy the ease of preparation. These salads are filling enough to be a light dinner.

Grilled Beef and Cabbage Salad

Stir-fried Beef and Spinach Salad

Tea-Smoked Salmon, Grilled Satay Chicken Tenders,
or Quick Char Siu served with Wo Ti's Garlicky Romaine Salad

HAVING COMPANY?

A quick and easy dinner party is possible. Here are a few suggestions for a variety of occasions.

COCKTAIL PARTY

Almost everything can be prepared in advance. Just heat the edamame and meatballs when your guests arrive, then enjoy the party.

Ho Chi Mojito

Yan's Cocktail Nuts

Edamame Appetizer

Cool Shrimp with Chili Dipping Sauce

Southeast Asian Meatballs

ELEGANT DINNER PARTY

Enjoy the nuts during the cocktail hour, then sit down to a delicious meal.

Yan's Cocktail Nuts

Crab and Asparagus Soup

Poached Halibut over Soba Noodles

Caramelized Asian Pears over Coconut Ice Cream

BACKYARD BARBECUE

A Yan family favorite activity. Invite your neighbors and you'll surprise them with a great meal.

Harvest Vegetables with Curry Dip

Backyard Asian Coleslaw

Dynasty Burgers with Easy and Tangy Sichuan Pickled Cucumbers

purchased taro chips

Lychee Lemonade

THE BIG GAME

Who doesn't love to watch the big game? If you serve these dishes, your house will be the place to go.

Peppery Chicken Wings

Honey-Glazed Spareribs

Sweet Soy–Braised Chicken Drummettes

Refreshing Beer Drink

INDEX

TABLE OF EQUIVALENTS

The exact equivalents in the following tables have been rounded for convenience.

LIQUID/DRY MEASURES

U.S.	METRIC	
1/4 teaspoon	1.25	milliliters
1/2 teaspoon	2.5	milliliters
1 teaspoon	5	milliliters
1 tablespoon (3 teaspoons)	15	milliliters
1 fluid ounce (2 tablespoons)	30	milliliters
1/4 cup	60	milliliters
1/3 cup	80	milliliters
1/2 cup	120	milliliters
1 cup	240	milliliters
1 pint (2 cups)	480	milliliters
1 quart (4 cups, 32 ounces)	960	milliliters
1 gallon (4 quarts)	3.84	liters
1 ounce (by weight)	28	grams
1 pound	454	grams
2.2 pounds	1	kilogram

LENGTH

U.S.	METRIC	
1/8 inch	3	millimeters
1/4 inch	6	millimeters
1/2 inch	12	millimeters
1 inch	2.5	centimeters

OVEN TEMPERATURE

FAHRENHEIT	CELSIUS	GAS
250	120	1/2
275	140	1
300	150	2
325	160	3
350	180	4
375	190	5
400	200	6
425	220	7
450	230	8
475	240	9
500	260	10